T0166610

LULA AND THE WORKERS PARTY
IN BRAZIL

LULA AND THE WORKERS PARTY IN BRAZIL

SUE BRANFORD AND
BERNARDO KUCINSKI
WITH HILARY WAINWRIGHT

THE NEW PRESS

NEW YORK
LONDON

Published in the United States by The New Press, New York, 2005
First published as *Politics Transformed: Lula and the Workers' Party in Brazil* by
Latin America Bureau, London, 2003
Distributed by W. W. Norton & Company, Inc., New York

LIBRARY OF CONGRESS CATALOGING-IN-PUBLICATION DATA

Branford, Sue.
    [Politics transformed]
    Lula and the Workers Party in Brazil / Sue Branford and Bernardo Kucinski,
with Hilary Wainwright.
        p. cm.
    First ed. has title: Politics transformed.
    Includes bibliographical references.
    ISBN 1-56584-866-7 (hc.)
    ISBN 1-56584-984-1 (pbk.)
        1. Partido dos Trabalhadores (Brazil)   2. Lula, 1945–   3. Brazil—Politics
and   government—1985–   I. Kucinski,   Bernardo.   II.   Wainwright,   Hilary.
III. Title.
JL2498.T7B72 2004
324.281'074—dc22   2003059323

The New Press was established in 1990 as a not-for-profit alternative to the large,
commercial publishing houses currently dominating the book publishing industry.
The New Press operates in the public interest rather than for private gain, and is
committed to publishing, in innovative ways, works of educational, cultural, and
community value that are often deemed insufficiently profitable.

www.thenewpress.com

Book design and composition by Westchester Book Group

Printed in the United States of America

2 4 6 8 10 9 7 5 3 1

CONTENTS

PREFACE

THE IDEA OF writing this book arose on the wave of delight that swept over many of us in October 2002 when we realized that at last, on his fourth attempt, Lula was going to be elected President of Brazil. For several years there had been loud rumblings of discontent in Latin America at the social cost of the Washington Consensus, the name given to the free-market economic policies that, with the encouragement of the international financial community, almost all governments in the region had been pursuing with unswerving conviction for up to two decades. The fact that Brazil, the regional giant, with a larger population than the rest of the countries in the continent put together, had elected its first working-class President on a program of far-reaching social change, was the most dramatic sign yet that the regional unrest could pave the way to the construction of a real alternative to neo-liberalism.

However, to the astonishment of his followers, Lula's government opted for conservative economic policies, with strict adherence to IMF rules, and even introduced some of the neo-liberal reforms that the Workers Party had formerly resisted (although stopping short of further privatizing state companies). At the beginning, almost everyone in the party believed that Lula had chosen this route out of political cleverness. As a leader with a track record as a radical, he was under permanent threat of destabilization by the right. If he started off with a clearly leftist agenda, it was thought, his chances of survival would be minimal, whereas if he began with conservative policies, he could strengthen his position and then, at some stage in the future, veer to the left (particularly if he kept his ties with the left, as he did).

At first, this version seemed to be borne out by events: Lula's

concern with the plight of the poor, repeatedly expressed during his
first two years in government, was clearly genuine; and he maintained links with social movements, including the MST (Brazil's
landless movement), which he continued to defend, despite strong
pressure from the conservative press, which wanted him to repress
the movement for what it saw as its illegal attack on the "sacred
right of private property."

As the months went by and nothing changed, a new theory was
developed to explain his submission to the diktat of big capital. This
theory reckoned that winning an election was not enough to change
substantially the balance of power in Brazil: one still had to fight
every inch of the way, not only to gain power within the state machinery, but also to win middle-class support for proposed changes
in public policies. And all this in an environment in which the media
was very hostile and the state structure was, in itself, an arena of
class struggle. However, given time, changes would occur. This, at
least, was the theory.

Now, however, after more than two years of PT government, the
dominant view within the party is that Lula's neo-liberal policies
were not just an imposition from outside nor a tactical option to
last only until he felt strong enough and confident enough to implement change, but rather, that Lula made an ideological option
and that his policies will not change. As a result, Lula will not substantially alter the structure of power in Brazil, far less "change Brazil" (as so many in the party had hoped). The left now defines Lula's
government as "social-liberal" — social on account of some important programs it is implementing to help the poor, and liberal due
to its adherence to the neo-liberal view on how the economy should
be run.

When he was at the Third World Social Forum in Porto Alegre
in southern Brazil in January 2003, Lula, who was just beginning
his government, was heralded as the leader of the resistance against
neo-liberalism. Two years later at the Fifth World Social Forum in
January 2005, also held in Porto Alegre, he was no longer seen as a
solution in the struggle against neo-liberalism, but as part of the

problem. Indeed, Lula's two-year experiment was seen as additional evidence of the strength of world financial capital and its grip on political structures worldwide. In that forum, Hugo Chávez, the combative president of Venezuela, replaced Lula as the dominant left-wing Latin American icon.

So these now are the main questions to be posed. Why has it happened this way? Was it inevitable? Is neo-liberalism indeed an inevitable stage of capitalism, impossible to be resisted, despite all the obvious evils it brings to society, including a very high level of unemployment? And what has happened to the Workers Party? With Lula's victory, a large number of party cadres, and in particular trade union leaders, were appointed to high positions within the state machinery. Others remained in their union strongholds but were co-opted through much easier access to state favors and facilities. Even the militant MST has to a large extent become dependent on government support.

The left wing of the party feels extremely uneasy. Some activists have already left the party and, in doing so, have weakened social movements. In the first edition of this book we posed the question of whether the Workers Party was an "outdated" manifestation of Marxist-inspired political action or the precursor of a new kind of political organization. Gaining power turned this rather academic question into a real and pressing issue, one that will continue to dominate the party's internal debate. Lula's shift toward conservatism has created a big gap between the government and the party. As it developed into a large political organization, the Workers Party accumulated great experience in the struggle for social reform, human rights, workers' rights, women's rights, and sustainable development. All this is incompatible with neo-liberalism.

Most probably the party leadership will attempt a kind of *aggiornamento*, the process of modernization and ideological change that emptied the Communist Party in Italy, and to a lesser degree other communist parties in Europe and elsewhere, of their class content and transformation drive. But social conditions in Latin America are not the same as in Europe. In Latin America, social inequality is far deeper and conflicts are much more acute. It is a stage set for revolution rather than mild social reform.

Another interesting question is: what happened to Lula? Instead of Lula changing Brazil, it seems it is Lula who has changed. This book shows how, before winning the presidency, he had already made history in Brazil, first by leading the strikes in the 1970s that paved the way for the military regime losing power, and then again by creating the unique political organization which is the Workers Party. Did Lula betray his origins and the ideals of a just society? At that Fifth Social Forum, the writer and activist Tariq Ali called Lula "the Tony Blair of the tropics." But this is rather a gross simplification. Although some of Lula's speeches suggest that he was seduced by the establishment and has surrendered to their arguments, his closest associates are convinced that he remains deeply committed to the plight of the poor and to people's empowerment. But, they point out, he has always been conservative in mentality and habits. He was made into a revolutionary by the circumstances of the 1970s and 1980s.

Some of Lula's improvised metaphors seem to corroborate this interpretation. For instance, when he claimed during his first year in office that one has to "put the house in order" before doing anything, or when he said during his second year in office, when his hands were already tied by the budget cuts imposed by the IMF, that "like in any family one cannot spend more than one earns." These and other humdrum images used by Lula suggest strongly— and this is perhaps why they are so disturbing—that Lula's administration lacks quality and courage. Besides making the mistake of comparing the management of a nation to that of a household, Lula presents shortcomings as virtues: lack of initiative is described as prudence. In the same way, he presents his decision not to challenge the socially unjust tariffs for public services—charged by multinational companies because of the very generous contracts they were granted by the previous government—as "respectability" in honoring contracts. And so on and so on.

This does not mean that the Lula government has failed to

achieve anything. Many members of the Workers Party, particularly those in government, claim that despite the grip of the banks on the running of the economy, the government is implementing many advanced social policies, and that in some areas it is even turning traditional structures upside down. The two most important social programs are, by far, Land Reform and the Family Support Program (Bolsa Familia). The land reform program is not new but was given more emphasis by Lula. Technical assistance and crop financing are also being offered to families through the Pronaf program. About 70,000 families were given land in 2003 and another 90,000 in 2004. This was a bitter disappointment to the MST, which had helped draw up a program for settling one million families over a three-year period, but the government is right when it claims that the quality of the technical and financial assistance given to the newly settled families has improved markedly. The Bolsa Familia, which is a development of the earlier Zero Hunger campaign, already benefits 6.5 million families, about half of the total number of families living under the poverty line. More recently Lula introduced Proui, a program to allow young people from lower middle class or poor families, who were unable to get a place in state universities, to study in private colleges. Other important initiatives are the national campaign against slave labor and the creation of a program of microcredit at low interest rates for wage-earners and the self-employed. The government is also in the vanguard of the struggle against Microsoft's monopoly on computer software and is planning to introduce nonproprietary software in state systems.

But all these progressive public policies are fragmented initiatives, which are unable alone to annul the overall neo-liberal character of the government's macroeconomic policies. The total transfer of income made by Bolsa Familia and Pronaf is about 5 billion reales (US$1.9 billion) a year, as compared with 180 billion reales (US$69.2 billion) a year transferred to the banks through the policy of excessively high interest rates. As we show in chapter one, it is only on the foreign-policy front that Lula's government has changed paradigms and taken very bold initiatives. Some hoped that these foreign-policy efforts would enhance the domestic agenda, but instead the reverse has been true; the bankers' grip on the domestic economy is dampening the prospects for foreign policy—particularly with respect to the delicate question of expressing open support for Nestor Kirchner, the president of Argentina, who is taking on the foreign bankers, and Hugo Chávez. Lula's apparent timidity in the face of the military is also disturbing. He hesitated for far too long before finally agreeing to open to the public the archives containing records of human rights abuses committed during the military dictatorship. As this paperback edition is being prepared in February 2005, the single somewhat forlorn hope that Lula will return to his origins lies in Lula himself: in his political instincts and his sensitivity toward the poor.

We have updated this book by writing this new introduction and by expanding Chapter 1, which in the hardback edition was already updated after Lula's first six months in office. The interviews with President Lula; José Dirceu, head of the President's political office; and Luiz Dulci, Lula's general secretary, were conducted at that time.

We would like to express our gratitude to Alfredo Saad Filho and to Harry Shutt for reading the manuscript and coming up with corrections and insightful suggestions. All views expressed and any remaining errors are, of course, the sole responsibility of the authors.

Bernardo Kucinski and Sue Branford
7 February 2005

LULA'S CHALLENGE

Sue Branford and Bernardo Kucinski

SÃO PAULO'S *AVENIDA PAULISTA* is a monument to money, the wide avenue is lined with the solid concrete and glass towers of giant banking corporations.[1] But on election night, on 27 October 2002, a sea of red flags lapped at the doors of the banks as thousands of supporters of the victorious PT (Partido dos Trabalhadores, or Workers Party) waited for their hero, chanting campaign slogans. When he appeared on a giant screen making his acceptance speech, men and women wept with joy—and disbelief. Was this really happening? After thirteen years and three failed attempts to win the presidency, was Luiz Inácio Lula da Silva really President of Brazil? Had the left wing finally come to power after 500 years of rule by the elite, the military, the landowners, and the bankers?

About 3,000 kilometers to the north, in the poverty-stricken rural hamlet of Caetés in the interior of the state of Pernambuco, people poured out into the streets as soon as the election result was announced on television. Old people hugged one another. Young people danced around the *trio elétrico* (a procession float), decked out in the Workers Party's distinctive red flags, as it made its way through the streets, blaring Carnival music. Fireworks went off. Here in the so-called Republic of the Silvas nearly everyone carries the surname and is—or at least claimed to be that night—a relative of the new President. "We never thought it would happen," said a cousin, fifty-three-year-old José Ricardo Silva. "We just dreamed it would, like we dream each year for rain."

Lula was born in Caetés in 1945, on 6 October (also the date of the first round of the 2002 election) according to his birth certificate, or on 27 October (the date of the second round of the election) according to his mother, Eurídice Ferreira de Mello, who died twenty years ago. When Lula was seven years old, his mother got into a *pau-de-arara* (open lorry) with her eight children and made the thirteen-day journey down to São Paulo to find work. Lula made the return journey to Caetés in 2002. "Almost nothing's changed," he said. "The same backwardness, the same corrupt politics that have always plagued this region."

In the days following the election Lula was mobbed wherever he went. Papers ran stories about "Saint Lula," and people began to idolize the man who, like millions of other Brazilians, had begun life in abject poverty, but was now President-elect of the world's fourth largest democracy and tenth largest economy. Yet Lula was constantly disassociating himself from Brazil's long tradition of powerful messianic leaders: the Workers Party he helped found in the early 1980s deliberately set out to limit the power of its leaders and to make them accountable to the mass of party members, who by 2002 numbered about 600,000. The PT had not found all the answers, for there was still an uneasy tension between the party itself and its administrations, which necessarily had to rule for the whole population, but it had gone much further than almost any other political party in the world toward making itself truly democratic.

The PT government was widely seen as the most exciting political development in Latin America since the election of the Marxist Salvador Allende, in Chile in 1970, and its progress was watched closely throughout the world. Lula's victory came at a time when the region, which for more than two decades had been dutifully and painfully implementing the IMF's neo-liberal reforms, was coming alive to protest again. In Venezuela Hugo Chávez—who, unlike Lula, does indeed project himself as the "savior of the poor"—was somewhat unexpectedly elected to power in December 1998 because of widespread disillusion with old, corrupt political parties. However, despite his success in routing the divided and inept opposition, Chávez faced an uphill struggle in his crusade to redistribute income and break the power of the moneyed elites, largely because he lacked the support of a solid and self-sustaining political party like the PT. In Bolivia, Evo Morales, an Aymara indigenous leader running on a strongly anti-neo-liberal program, came close to winning the presidential elections in August 2002. He was defeated, but the mass support that had nearly catapulted him into office was expressed a year later in the popular uprising that forced out of office the neo-liberal president Sánchez de Lozada. And in Ecuador a coalition of indigenous groups and left-wing movements had won the presidential elections on 20 October 2002 in a remarkable setback for the traditional political parties. In Argentina, the spectacular collapse of the neo-liberal project in December 2001 had led to the emergence of exciting new forms of local participatory democracy, such as the *asambleas populares* (popular assemblies) and the factory takeovers by workers. Although these were not replicated on a national scale, President Néstor Kirchner, who came to office in May 2003, seemed committed to introducing important political and economic reforms. Particularly welcome for the PT was the importance he was giving to strengthening Mercosul, the regional trade bloc. Against this background of simmering discontent, the PT's victory in Brazil's presidential election was clearly the biggest gain for the left up to that point. If the PT could successfully break out of the constraints it had inherited from the Cardoso government, then Brazil could lead a continent-wide search for a real alternative to neo-liberalism. But could the PT achieve this? Or had it made so many concessions, first to gain power and then to govern, that it had effectively relinquished any chance of carrying out this historic role?

In the run-up to the election, the PT reinvented itself as a moderate left-wing party. In 1998, shortly after his third defeat in the presidential race, Lula made it clear to the PT national leadership that he would agree to run a fourth time only if he were given a free hand to form alliances across the political board and was provided with the resources to run a slick, professional electoral campaign. The new strategy, which Lula devised with the PT's president, José Dirceu (who spent the late 1960s as an urban guerrilla and who was sprung from jail by the spectacular kidnapping of the U.S. ambassador in Rio), was endorsed by the leadership and then rigorously enforced. The PT ran an all-inclusive presidential campaign in which, with the support of some sugary and politically dubious TV commercials built around the slogan "Lula, Peace, and Love," it sought to win over those sectors of society that had traditionally been hostile to it, particularly the business community. It selected Senator José Alencar from the small right-of-center Liberal Party as Lula's running mate. Alencar, who owned Brazil's largest textile company, Coteminas, and had a personal fortune of about US$500 million, was progressive to the extent that he paid his workers a decent wage—at least by Brazilian standards—and allowed them to form independent unions, and was nationalist, but he was still clearly part of the business establishment.

Many of the PT's oldest supporters, above all left-wing intellectuals, were horrified at what they perceived as a deeply compromised and cosmetic makeover, particularly because the Liberal Party was closely linked to the socially conservative evangelical Universal Church of the Kingdom of God. "It's no secret that, at first, I was against the alliance with the Liberal Party," said Antônio Cândido, a leading intellectual and one of the founders of the Workers Party, in an interview in mid-2002.[2]

> Lula even mentioned the fact that both I and Marilena Chauí [a lecturer in philosophy at the University of São Paulo and culture secretary in the first PT administration in São Paulo] were opposed, in an interview with the *Folha de S. Paulo*. Lula said that, while we were intellectuals, he was a politician and had to follow another logic. But then, after the decision, I accepted it. I think it's so important for Brazil that Lula wins this election that I'll accept any alliance that he deems necessary. And I'm still confident that, once elected, he and the party will change this country.

Lula's strategy worked, in that it delivered electoral victory. Old opponents were won over. Eugênio Staub, chief executive of a leading hi-fi company, Gradiente, decided to back Lula publicly, even though he was a close friend of the other main candidate, José Serra, and had earlier said that he would vote for him. He made his decision after holding several secret meetings with Lula. "Serra is a competent and very intelligent man, but the international moment is extremely critical for Brazil," he explained. "We need someone in the presidency who is 100 percent a politician. And Lula is a real statesman. He is the only person who can unite labor, business, and other broad social sectors. And that's what Brazil needs today."[3] Millions came to the same conclusion as Staub, and voted for a man they had rejected in the past. Lula won the second round of the elections with a large majority. Afterward he commented that he had won just as he had always dreamed of winning: in a clean contest without personal abuse or dirty tricks.

Lula's victory was greeted with delight at home and abroad. "I think Lula's triumph is a key moment in Brazil's history, like the abolition of slavery or the proclamation of the Republic," commented Francisco de Oliveira, a leading sociologist. "It may be the point at which we move on from a passive history, in which the country is led by the dominant blocs, to an active history in which the dominated classes have a big impact on state policies."

"The result of the election is important, not just for Brazil, but for the rest of the world," said Boaventura de Sousa Santos, economics professor at the University of Coimbra in Portugal. "With the coming to power of the Workers Party, Brazil is finally completing the long transition from the twenty-one years of military rule." And the British historian Eric Hobsbawm commented: "The PT's victory is one of the few events at the beginning of the twenty-first century that gives us hope for the rest of the century. The PT is a new force in the history of Brazil."[4]

But the euphoria didn't last long. "We are in government but not in power. Power today is global power, the power of big companies, the power of financial capital," said Lula's close aide, the Dominican friar Frei Betto, somewhat defensively, when Lula's government had completed five months in office amidst widespread complaints that he had betrayed his promises, that instead of cre-

ating 8 million jobs in four years, his policies had already destroyed
a further half a million jobs in just five months. A year later, part
of the jobs lost were recovered as the economy began timidly to
grow again, but Frei Betto left the government anyway, convinced
that Lula had abandoned his ideals. "I thought our ship was sailing
east, but instead it sailed west," he said rather metaphorically.

The first half of Lula's administration was marked by severe cuts
in the budget and highly recessionary monetary policies in strict
obedience to the IMF's diktat. It was the opposite of what Lula had
promised during his campaign. PT militants were astonished by
Lula's decision to hand over the Central Bank and some other key
areas of the economy, such as exports and agriculture production,
to bankers and other representatives of the *ancien régime*. The alliance between the left and the center, envisaged in the first draft of
the Workers Party manifesto, was replaced by an alliance with conservative forces.

In an exclusive interview for this book, Luiz Dulci, a former trade
union leader close to Lula who helped to write that original manifesto and who is now the president's general secretary, said that the
decision to change course was traumatic.

> We suffered, not because we were forced to change our
> views, for we weren't. Our aims remain the same. We
> want to achieve fast economic growth and to redistribute
> income so we can put an end to the high level of in-
> equality that prevails in Brazil. We want to push ahead
> with our program of structural reforms, to be imple-
> mented through negotiations and taking into consider-
> ation the degree of complexity reached by the Brazilian
> economy. Our suffering comes from having to put mon-
> etary stability before our program and having to use the
> classic instruments of monetary austerity. We didn't pre-
> pare ourselves for a period of transition.

It had already become clear during the last few months of the campaign that it would be necessary to forestall a speculative attack on the national currency, which could destroy any chances of success by Lula's administration, even before it started. In June the mega-speculator George Soros had said that Brazil would face economic meltdown if it elected Lula. Big capital, it seemed, was betting on Lula's defeat. Several foreign newspapers described Lula as a "left-wing populist," close to Hugo Chávez and Fidel Castro, and some right-wing Miami papers even included him as part of the "axis of evil." José Serra, the other leading presidential candidate, added to the climate of panic by warning that Brazil, under Lula, could become another Argentina—referring to the deep and generalized crisis that hit the neighboring country's economy and political system in 2002 after the government had gone bankrupt. Opinion polls undertaken by Lula's staff showed that the fear of an Argentine-style crisis was widespread, particularly among the poor and the lower middle class.

Two months before polling day, in response to what was by then seen by the Workers Party as "financial terrorism" by big capital to influence the outcome of the elections, Lula issued a "Letter to the Brazilian People," in which, while reiterating his promise to change the country's economic policies, he said he intended at the same time to respect existing contracts and commitments, which was a way of saying that his government was not going to default on the foreign debt or, for that matter, on the even larger domestic debt.

By January 2003, when Lula was sworn into office, the national currency, the *real,* had lost 30 percent of its value against the dollar in just a couple of months, and some rating agencies were putting "Brazil risk" at over 1300 points, one of the highest rates in the world, which meant that the foreign debt certificates issued by the Brazilian government (the so-called C bonds) were traded on the speculative secondary market with an interest rate of 13 percentage points above that of U.S. Treasury bills. Over US$6 billion in hot money left the country in just three months. Even revolving credit lines provided by foreign banks for Brazilian exports, which had the guarantee of the goods that were being exported, were not being renewed. Pressure by foreign capital was not only rhetorical, it was also material.

The prediction of chaos made by George Soros was becoming a typical self-fulfilling prophecy. Luiz Dulci explained how Lula's staff had assessed the situation: "We reckoned that the chronic financial instability, now reaching a new peak, had disorganized the Brazilian economy to such an extent that it was having an impact on social behavior and public morality. The country had not only lost international credibility, but also confidence in itself. It was becoming a plaything in the hands of world speculators."

This was the background to the decision by Lula and his closest advisers to hand over the running of the Central Bank to the bankers themselves — although under the direction of a high-ranking and long-standing PT cadre, Antonio Palocci, who became finance minister. The rationale for this decision was that a financial disaster at the start of Lula's government would mean disaster for his entire term in office, while initial austerity policies could always be changed later into expansionist ones. The agreement with the IMF was quickly reaffirmed, and the target for the public-sector surplus, required to pay the debt installments, was set at an even higher level (4.25 percent of GDP) than the one demanded by the IMF. This was designed to produce a "credibility shock" among foreign investors and to appease speculators and banks.

A month later, Lula also introduced a 45 percent, across-the-board budget cut, which affected most programs, including social ones. The credibility shock worked well on the foreign front, reversing the outflow of capital. Praise for Lula's austerity policies came from all conservative quarters. But a parallel "loss-of-credibility shock" rocked the confidence in Lula felt by left-wing intellectuals and economists, as well as many PT supporters. Lula himself went through an initial period of anguish in which he could barely sleep, visibly tormented by doubts.

As time went by, the conservative figures in the Central Bank gained a degree of political autonomy and went for a policy of confrontation vis-à-vis the government itself. It was this that led Frei Betto to state where real power lay—in the hands of big capital. The Central Bank under Lula not only kept interest rates at a high level, but even increased them a month later by another 2.5 points to 26.5 percent, making them the highest in the world. By May 2003, unemployment in São Paulo, the country's largest metropolitan area, reached the all-time record level of 20.6 percent. Inflation was forced down, but at the cost of wiping out economic growth during the first year of Lula's term.

The second year was marked by economic recovery stimulated by strong demand for Brazilian commodities from China and elsewhere and productivity gains by Brazilian companies, as wages in the manufacturing industry declined on average by about 7 percent. Lula could claim that his economic policies were proving successful, but interest rates were still the highest in the world. As a result, the cost of servicing the public debt was much higher than it had been in the first year, which meant that the budget had to be severely cut yet again, which damaged all social programs.

Dissatisfaction spread even wider, in particular among the PT's rank and file, threatening the very unity of the party. Many said that Lula had changed, that he had sold out to the bankers. They pointed out that high interest rates were inconsistent with the desired aim of reducing the public debt, and that the only clear rationale for maintaining the rates at such a high level was to guarantee the reproduction of the system, the perpetual submission of the country to the creditors of the public debt.

Ministers in charge of social programs, people like Olívio Dutra, who was responsible for dealing with urban problems, such as the massive shortfall of 7 million homes and the serious water and sewage shortages, complained in a quiet voice that they lacked money for even the most basic tasks—for public works that the President himself had promised, during his trips to poor urban neighborhoods and to the interior, would be undertaken. The land reform minister, Miguel Rossetto, also complained about a lack of money for land expropriation and settlements.

On several occasions during those two years, PT federal deputies or PT militants launched manifestos in which they demanded an immediate end to recessionary policies. "If this is not done immediately, we may never be able to recover," said Ivan Valente, the federal deputy who organized the first such manifesto. The day before, former PT president José Dirceu, now head of the President's political office and the most powerful man in the government (after Lula), was heckled when trying to persuade an assembly of public-sector workers in São Paulo, mostly supporters of the Workers Party, that Lula's proposal for a reform of the Social Security system was just and necessary. "Liars, liars," they shouted. "This is the reform being asked for by Brazil's creditors and the IMF."

It was precisely at this tense moment that Lula gave an interview for this book in which he answered all questions calmly and even wittily. It was evident that by then all his anguish had gone. Self-assured and relaxed, he conveyed the feeling that he knew very well what was going on, that he was in full command, and that all he was asking for was a little more patience.

> Some people say that I have changed, but I haven't. It is the situation that has changed. When you get married, you change. You tell your friends you will continue meeting them, doing the same things as before, but it isn't true. You have a wife, a family, and a house to take care of. When the Workers Party was born, it was a tiny baby. It grew up, became a teenager, then an adult, then it got married, and with marriage came the responsibility of governing. The time for talking, for saying "I think, I believe, I wish, I oppose," has gone. Now it is the time for doing. This doesn't mean that I've changed my ideology or betrayed the party. I still believe in everything

I've always believed in. I still have my dreams, but one has to live in reality. We moved into a house that was in shambles. We have to put in a new roof and a new floor. We have to redecorate, and then we have to adapt the house to our needs. This all takes time.

We all knew during the election campaign that the country was in bad shape. But when we had access to the real figures, we discovered that the situation was far more difficult than we had thought. For instance, we discovered that about 14 billion reales [US$5 billion] had been allocated to various programs without any indication in the budget of where this money was going to be found. We discovered that the previous administration had left 7 billion reales [US$2.5 billion] in unpaid bills. We found it had issued checks on the very last day it was in office, on 31 December.

We made a decision: to use the meager resources at our disposal as competently and as austerely as we could during this first year, which I am calling the Year of Tolerance, during which people must understand—and do understand—that I am busy putting the house in order. I'm confident because I'm an optimist by nature. People know from their own experience in life that beginnings are often difficult. It is like getting a job after you've been unemployed for a long time. The moment you start work, you have to start paying bills. And you have lots of bills to pay. People know that we are still paying bills left from the past.

Lula was referring indirectly to the growing support he was receiving at that time from ordinary people and voters. Opinion polls showed that about 85 percent of the population backed him, despite the increasing opposition he was facing from public employees and the left wing of the party, and despite the undeniable deterioration in the economic situation of the country. No other Brazilian president had ever received this level of support after five months in office.

Lula's election increased the self-esteem of Brazilians of all classes, including the very rich, and restored in them the desire to help and to participate, something that had disappeared a long time before. Highly sensitive to the mood of the people and convinced of the severity of the crisis, which meant that it would not be solved by cosmetic measures alone, Lula had been trying to gain as much time as possible. "Never before in our history have people discussed so intensely the solutions for our problems. Everybody wants to participate. If we behave in a ethical manner, if we root out corruption, if we explain the situation, people will understand and will give us time."

Lula said that on the following day he would be meeting old fellow workers from the car industry. He complained that the presidency tended to isolate him from the people and that he fought against this: "The poor, who elected me, want to shake my hand but are prevented from doing so by security guards, while people who opposed me during the campaign can easily arrange an interview in the presidential palace in order to ask the government to invest in this or that or to request some other favor."

In spite of his relative isolation, intrinsic to the position he occupies, Lula exerts more charisma on most Brazilians, in particular the poor, than he did as a candidate. One of the reasons for this is Lula's way of speaking, which has changed significantly since he became President. Almost every day he takes part in a ceremony and delivers a speech written beforehand by his staff, but on almost every occasion he departs from his text and improvises, resorting to parables, metaphors, and analogies based on ordinary people's lives, to explain the most complicated issues and problems. He is becoming a master of oratory with his own highly characteristic style. He also resorts frequently to the image of God. And he often compares his responsibility in government with that of a father toward a family. Commentators have compared his charisma with that of Getúlio Vargas, the dictator who ruled Brazil in the 1930s and was dubbed by the press then as the "Father of the Poor." Others say he is tapping into the messianic tradition in Brazilian politics (despite the PT's emphasis on collective leadership).

Lula does not do anything in politics without a reason, and he explains why he talks so much to the people, and through easily understandable parables. "One has to explain. In the most difficult situation, the President must talk to the people all the time. If a father has promised something to his son and is later unable to do it, he has to explain why. The President must keep in touch with the people all the time."

Luiz Dulci said that Lula's strength derives not only from the way he speaks, unprecedented in Brazilian politics, but also from his perseverance in going for the presidency again, after being defeated three times, and from the unexpected places he chose to visit, together with the little gestures he makes during his trips. All this conveys sincerity and authenticity, he said. Everything that was seen in him previously as a defect is now seen as a virtue.

> With his victory Lula underwent a mental process in which he freed himself from complexes he had earlier and acquired a far more universal personality than that of a former metalworkers' leader. He now identifies most with poor people, while earlier his main reference point was with organized workers. He has also recovered his dimension as a man who originally came from the dramatic, poverty-stricken northeast of Brazil. His speeches today express anguish with the state of humanity, a high level of spirituality. A strong bond has developed between ordinary people and Lula, which is far more intense than anything one could have predicted. His life story has become a symbol of spirituality. It has gone very deep under people's skin.

However, Luiz Dulci believed that the main reason for the support that Lula was receiving from the population, even though he had postponed the fulfillment of his campaign promises, came from the reckoning, in particular by the poor, that Brazil had reached the very bottom of a crisis and that the reconstruction of the country required prudence and that it was, indeed, necessary to put the house in order first.

> The educated left thinks this is only rhetoric, but the poor, who feel in their own flesh the hardness of life, are prudent by nature and totally agree with Lula's approach. They feel that they took a very big step in putting him there, in the presidency, and they still feel a little insecure, and for this reason they prefer prudence. It is a kind of unwritten intimate pact between Lula and millions of Brazilians who never belonged to the Workers Party, people who now hope that Lula will take Brazil out of this messy situation. They do not want it to go wrong. They keep writing to us, sending messages warning Lula to be cautious, to do only what is possible at each stage, to beware of the traps set by the big shots, by people who are always close to government.

However, after two years in office, support for Lula has declined to about 60 percent. This is still high, given the situation, and can largely be attributed to Lula's continuing charisma, but it is not at a record level anymore. And the PT's defeat in the municipal elections in November 2004, not only in its former showcase, Porto Alegre, but also in São Paulo, Brazil's largest city, can be attributed in part to disenchantment with the Lula government.

Very pragmatic, but guided by some fundamental ethical principles, Lula developed a new style of governing, based on intense negotiations with the aim of reaching consensual solutions, with the involvement of all sectors of society, irrespective of political parties, social class, or anything else. He created several councils, the most

important being the Social Development Council, coordinated at
first by the former mayor of Porto Alegre, Tarso Genro, the creator
of the participatory budget (see Chapter 5). The inspiration for these
councils was the Spanish Council, created during the transition from
dictatorship to democracy, with the participation of trade unions
and employers, to discuss reforms in taxation and the social welfare
system.

But the council went into slow decline, as most of the arguments
from industry and trade unions on how to achieve development
were not listened to by the finance minister, Antonio Palocci, who
was totally committed to the views of the banking sector. Tarso
Genro became education minister and the council was put under
coordination of the lesser-known labor minister, Jaques Wagner. At
the end of 2004, Palocci dared to submit to the council a study that
claimed to prove that one of the reasons for high interest rates in
Brazil was the existence of state banks, such as the National Economic and Social Development Bank (BNDES), which channeled
certain savings, compulsorily deducted from workers' wages, into
the financing of development projects and popular housing. The
logical conclusion of this argument would be to dismantle the entire
system of compulsory workers' savings, state banks, and popular
housing and sanitation programs. In short, to implement the neo-
liberal agenda.

Lula's views on democracy are a far cry from the Latin American
authoritarian tradition: he says democracy is an intense and contin-
uous process of negotiations in which all parts have legitimate points
of view.

> A negotiated solution is always better than a law passed
> by a majority against the wish of a minority. There is no
> point imposing solutions out of my own head. I have to
> put forward a proposal to society and then let people
> discuss it. People obey a good agreement better than the
> law. My ministers have been to Congress to debate their
> proposals eleven times so far. I myself have been twice

in this short period of time. Never before in Brazil's history has a president held so many meetings with so many sectors of society.

Despite all the economic limitations imposed by Brazil's financial vulnerability, and despite strong criticism by the ruling elite, Lula is maintaining and even expanding the program launched on the very day his victory was announced, which has changed Brazil's political scene and is the main reason why so many people still identify with him. Called initially the Zero Hunger program, it has now turned into a program of subsidies for poor families and has been given a new name, Bolsa Familia (Family Stock Market)—but the intention remains the same—to guarantee three meals a day to every Brazilian. It is estimated that 20 million Brazilians, including a large number of children and young mothers, actually go hungry and that another 20 million suffer from some degree of malnutrition. This means that about 25 percent of the Brazilian population is not eating and drinking properly. The new program touched a taboo and, along with strong support, provoked equally strong hostility, largely because it undermines the very foundation of the political control exercised by local oligarchies in the poorest areas of the interior. But international reaction was immediate and positive, and the program is already changing the way the World Bank and IMF think on this issue. It was this more than anything else that led to Lula being rapidly recognized as a new—and perhaps the main—leader today of the Third World. Luiz Dulci explains:

> The Zero Hunger program was the result of an extraordinary intuition by the President. He wanted something more concrete for his acceptance speech. He proposed the issue of hunger. And, at the moment he was delivering the speech, he changed the scale of his intervention. He created a political symbol and a cause that brings together the emergency dimension with the structural dimension. It is also a universal cause. At the

beginning we did not realize the conceptual problems
involved and even now we have been unable to structure
the program in an adequate manner. But the Zero Hunger program was what changed the agenda, burying neo-
liberalism.

Lula has also launched a bold foreign policy of rapprochement
with India, China, Africa, and Latin America. An entire tradition of
independent foreign policy, which was dormant at Brazil's presti-
gious Foreign Ministry, has come to life with great energy. In a very
short period of time, Brazil led the move to create the Friends of
Venezuela group, which was instrumental in preventing a second
attempted coup against Chávez, revived the Mercosul initiative as a
means of facing pressure from Washington for a U.S.–dominated
common market, and struck several trade agreements with neighboring countries, including a free-trade agreement between Mercosul and the Comunidad Andina (Andean Community). Brazil has
established a timetable with Argentina for setting up a complete
system of common external tariffs by the end of 2006. It has created
a new and powerful desk at the Foreign Ministry to advance relations with Latin America. And it has used the National Economic
and Social Development Bank (BNDES) to open credit lines with
neighboring countries, with the aim of boosting regional trade.

Lula has attempted to do this without offending the U.S. government. On the contrary, he wants to show the Bush administration that a people's democracy, based on strong parties and stable
economies, is the best antidote against terrorism. According to Luiz
Dulci, "Lula made a strategic option to pursue the democratization
of the international economic order, but we cannot do it by an
ideological approach. We must combine principles with national interests. Pragmatism with principles. And we must innovate in our
methods, as we did by creating the Friends of Venezuela group. We
have recovered the right to intervene in the world scene that was
lost by previous governments."

The next step will probably be a Brazilian initiative, perhaps with some help from Fidel Castro and even the U.S. government, to put an end to the Colombian internal war. But Lula's audacious foreign policy has already run into U.S. opposition, because Lula's ultimate aim is to integrate the entire subcontinent under Brazilian leadership. As one of the top members of the government put it: "Bolivia, Paraguay, and Uruguay are already totally dependent on Brazil. Mexico is lost, for it has become a colony of the United States. We need now to reach the other countries that are not members of Mercosul: Colombia, Venezuela, Ecuador, and Peru."

This is not rhetoric. It is a strategic project, designed by experienced diplomats, now under Lula's leadership. Instead of just blaming U.S. imperialism for all evils in the region, Lula wants action. This is the way he puts it:

> We had fifty years of the cold war and then neo-liberalism. This has all ended now. We are entering a new era. I want to introduce a new idea, the idea that South America is very important space but we have never devoted time and energy to getting it physically integrated. We are still separated by rivers two hundred feet wide, while it costs next to nothing to build a bridge. We have no roads, no railways linking our countries. We must launch an ambitious program to integrate Latin America.

As Lula reaches the halfway point of his four-year mandate, it is evident that some advances are being made. His government is slowly changing the face of public administration. For the first time in Brazil's history, union leaders have been put in charge of state companies' pension funds and members of the Landless Movement (MST) are becoming managers of regional offices of the Land Reform Ministry. For the first time a black person has been nominated a judge in the Supreme Court. Everywhere in government one can see former activists in the armed movement against the military dictatorship of the 1960s, occupying high positions. The state machinery is being slowly democratized. But there have also been important setbacks, as the ruling elite perceives these changes and fights back. Carlos Lessa, a leading economist with nationalist views, was sacked as president of the National Economic and Social Development Bank (BNDES) after a smearing campaign by the conservative press. A similar initiative led to the sacking of Clayton Campanhola, director of the leading state agricultural research institute, Embrapa. Not by coincidence, he refused support to the legalization of genetically modified soybeans, something that the government, after heavy pressure from the biotechnology multinational Monsanto, is slowly permitting.

Lula's surrendering to such pressure is very disturbing. Even more worrying is the feeling that there is a hidden neo-liberal agenda that is being slowly implemented. This means that, despite gains here and there, Lula is failing in his central promise to "change Brazil" for the benefit of the poor and disadvantaged.

There is still hope that he will change the course of the ship, if he wins a second term in office, which is highly probable. When asked about his promises to change Brazil, Lula still replies: "I'll not fail. I cannot fail. I'll do everything that has to be done but not in a rush. I'm aware that if I fail, it will not only be the failure of Lula but the defeat of a historical movement. It we fail, it will take another fifty years for the people to raise their heads again."

THE RISE OF THE WORKERS PARTY

Bernardo Kucinski

WHILE SOCIALISM DECLINED in the West during the final decades of the twentieth century, the Brazilian left created three new forms of popular organization that took the left by surprise in other countries. These were the Workers Party (PT), a new strong trade union confederation called *Central Única dos Trabalhadores* (CUT), and the nationwide Landless Workers Movement or *Movimento dos Trabalhadores Rurais Sem Terra* (MST). The Workers Party lay at the heart of these unprecedentedly large organizations, which not only shared similar dreams of social transformation but often the same members and leaders. After growing slowly at first, the PT suddenly won two consecutive unexpected victories at the beginning of the twenty-first century, first electing an impressive number of mayors in Brazil's major cities in 2000, and then, in 2002, first getting more members into Congress and into the state government assemblies than any other party, and then having its main leader and one of its founding members—the former metalworker Luiz Inácio Lula da Silva, nicknamed Lula—elected President of Brazil by a massive majority.

Lula's election had, above all, an emblematic dimension: it was the first time in Brazil's history—and in the history of Latin America since the Mexican revolution—that the son of a dispossessed peasant had reached the pinnacle of political power. The implications of his victory are far-reaching both within Brazil and without, as can be gauged by the size of the Brazilian economy (the tenth-largest in the world), the continental dimension of the country, and its strategic position in Latin America.

The prospect of a left-wing government in power in Brazil sent shivers down the spine of global finance. But it also raised great expectations among Brazil's voters, demoralized by two decades of neo-liberal policies that had destroyed much of Brazil's social fabric and taken unemployment and violence to unprecedented levels. Lula was not elected with a mandate to end capitalism, far less to do so by revolutionary means, but he was clearly elected with a mandate to completely change priorities in Brazil. The new concerns are to care for ordinary people, in particular the poor; to combat drug trafficking; to restore national dignity; and to implement public policies for housing, health, public transport, and education, sectors that during the neo-liberal era were either altogether neglected or subordinated to the priority of servicing the foreign and domestic debt and reducing the fiscal deficit.

The contradictions that emerged from neo-liberalism during the last years of the Cardoso government were so intense that Lula won with the backing of a substantial part of the middle classes, and even with a degree of support from the ruling elite. In fact, one of the many ironies of Lula's rise to power is that while concepts such as "social pact" were anathema at the birth of the Workers Party in 1980, Lula explicitly asked for the support of the ruling elite during his campaign and, immediately after his victory, he proposed the formation of such a pact between workers and employers, so that the country's problems could be resolved consensually. Even so, one of the questions his experiment in power will have to answer is the extent to which the ruling elite and the upper classes are prepared for compromise and will submit to the leadership of the Workers Party.

Will the United States' imperium, now in an era of expansion and reaffirmation of its rule worldwide, accept a left-wing government in power in Brazil, as part of a broader rejection of free-market economics in Latin America? Not only the PT, but other left and center-left parties expanded their influence in the 2002 elections. Lula should be able to negotiate majority support in both houses of Congress; the total number of seats held by the left in the federal Chamber of Deputies increased by 40 percent, from 112 to 161. Oligarchical and corrupt politicians were ousted in several parts of the country. There was a political revival and renewal of the left, which the conservative camp called the "red windfall." Combined with Lula's election with an impressive 57.2 million votes (over 61 percent of the votes cast), this development marks an important change in the balance of power in Brazil.

This process naturally attracted the attention of the world, particularly in Latin America, where most countries are undergoing one crisis or another, all of them very serious. The victory of Lula and the PT is being seen by the rest of the world, right and left alike, as perhaps the dawn of a new era, certainly the start of a new experiment in democracy. For Latin America, Lula's rise to power could pave the way for the development of alternative policies opposed to the monetarist recipes that have been imposed on the subcontinent by successive International Monetary Fund (IMF) missions since the start in 1982 of the foreign debt crisis, and have led to two decades of economic stagnation and social misery.

Argentineans, Peruvians, Bolivians, Venezuelans, Ecuadorians, and Cubans are seeing Lula's rise to power and his administration as a new experiment in radical democracy, an experiment that could give Latin America's formal democracies the social content they have so far lacked. For the left, Lula's victory paves the way for a new debate on the relationship between socialism and democracy, based on a real experiment in a big country. Lula and the PT's theoretical thinkers believe that the left has not yet developed a more comprehensive ideological answer to neo-liberal hegemony. They have won an election but they have not won power, in the sense of exerting hegemony. This hegemony still has to be built, by first changing the nature of the state apparatus, which is quite large and has been deployed since its creation by the Portuguese 500 years ago as an instrument of class domination. Particularly worrying for the PT is the domination by the right of Brazil's judiciary, which may prove more of a headache for the PT than Congress. The PT has only a four-year mandate to build a new hegemony to replace the current structure, while also changing the culture of Brazil's state bureaucracy.

Whatever the results of this experiment, Lula's 2002 election campaign will enter the history of democracy as a landmark and a case study of a people that decided to take destiny into their own hands. One of the reasons for Lula's defeat in three previous campaigns was that his opponents claimed he was not fit to rule because he lacked formal education. The majority of ordinary Brazilians, who also lack a comprehensive formal education and have known at least once or twice in their lives what it is like to go hungry or not to have the money to buy medicine, decided in 2002 not to submit to this argument, but to identify with Lula. This process raised the self-esteem of Brazilian voters and changed their mentality, defeating the established assumption that only the elite is entitled to rule. Lula was elected as the hero of a psychologically liberated Brazil. This has given him an extraordinary momentum and enviable political capital with which to start his government.

THE COMING OF AGE OF THE PT

The PT emerged in the wake of a series of major strikes in the late 1970s that mortally wounded the military dictatorship (which was then given the coup de grâce by huge nationwide mobilizations in 1983 and 1984 for the right to elect the country's president on a direct vote). The protagonists of the country's belated process of industrialization, the metalworkers, helped create and then led a party that also arrived late on the scene. The metalworkers' strikes occurred at a time when the military dictatorship was faltering. In 1975 Vladimir Herzog, a well-known television news editor, had been arrested and killed under torture at the notorious CODI–DOI headquarters of the security forces. Just a few months later, in January 1976, an industrial worker, Manoel Fiel Filho, died in similar circumstances. In 1977, students took to the streets. By then intellectuals were calling for an amnesty for political offenses and for the restoration of democracy. Meanwhile, new trade union leaders had emerged from under the protective cloak of the "liberation theology" wing of the Catholic Church and were rejecting the old trade-union structures that had been taken over by the employers. All these forces contributed to the creation of the PT.

When it was founded, the PT attracted traditionally incompatible groups, including Trotskyists, Leninists, Marxists, Catholics from the liberation wing of the Catholic Church, nearly illiterate workers, and renowned intellectuals. In just a few years this alliance of opposites managed to become the first mass party in Brazil with predominantly socialist ideas, and the only mainstream political party with activists and a life outside electoral periods. In fact, the PT had a level of activism as great as that of the old communist parties, which had operated clandestinely during most of their existence in Brazil and which, for this and other reasons, had developed a conspiratorial political culture. In contrast, from the very beginning the Workers Party held the view that politics must be exercised in the open, in the public sphere, and within a democratic framework.

For many years the PT remained a minor party. This was partly because the core of the working class that founded the party—the automobile industry workers—lost its vitality during the following decade. Even so, after a period of slow growth in electoral support in the years immediately following its foundation in 1980, the PT grew rapidly. In the municipal elections in November 1988, the last to be held under the old Constitution, the PT unexpectedly elected 36 mayors, including Luiza Erundina in São Paulo. The swing toward the PT may have been helped by public revulsion at the deaths of three workers after the army was sent in to break up a strike at the Volta Redonda steel mill. Then, in 1989, Lula came within an inch of winning the presidency at his first attempt. Instead, after a dirty political campaign, Fernando Collor de Mello, who came from a traditional ruling family from the northeast, won the election and was later forced out by massive mobilizations against his corruption. By the early 1990s, the PT was the strongest party on the Brazilian left, although it was still a minority voice in the country's overall political spectrum. By then the PT had local party committees in 3,600 towns with approximately 600,000 members, two-thirds of whom were regular participants in the party's activities, a grassroots militancy not found in other parties in Brazil. As early as 1988, the PT received 12.8 percent of the vote—almost as much as each of the three major center and right-wing parties—in the elections for the Federal Chamber of Deputies, which elects its members by a system of proportional representation. It also elected seven senators and 60 deputies in the Federal Congress, making it the fourth-largest party. The PT became a pole of attraction for Brazil's parliamentary opposition, consolidating its hegemony on the left.

However, the final years of the decade were not easy ones for the PT. With a significant increase in unemployment, the CUT, which had 20 million affiliates, lost some of its influence to the "business unionism" promoted by populist unions. The PT was also unable to capture the support of the middle classes, who were attracted by neo-liberal ideas and lost some ideological and organizational ground to Marxist parties, such as the PCdoB (Communist Party of Brazil) and the PSTU (Partido Socialista dos Trabalhadores Unificado), in the student movement. Later the PSTU joined the PT, but the PCdoB remained the dominant force among left-wing students. At the end of the 1990s, other groups of workers who had participated in the creation of the PT, such as bank clerks, were also greatly weakened by the technological revolution, industrial decline, and unemployment. The PT, however, did not disappear. On the contrary, it slowly continued to grow, gaining support from new sectors of society, such as the impoverished lower-middle class and other dissatisfied groups.

Then, in the municipal elections in 2000, the first landslide on a national scale took place, largely in response to growing disenchantment with Fernando Henrique Cardoso. Party candidates received approximately one-fifth of the votes (12 million) and gained control of many large cities, including some state capitals such as São Paulo, the world's third-largest metropolis. The breakthrough was largely due to the public perception of the PT as the only political force that was different. It was left wing, which the public viewed with greater receptivity as a result of increasing distrust of Cardoso's free-market reforms, particularly after the spectacular collapse of the currency, called the real, in late 1999. The PT was also the only party that included ethics as part of its political program (and put that program into practice in the municipalities in which it was in power). By then, the press had fully exposed the corruption inherent in the implementation of the neo-liberal model. By capitalizing on the public's disgust with corruption and with neo-liberalism in general, the PT received an avalanche of votes. These results changed the party's ranking in Brazilian politics and helped it to emerge in pole position in the 2002 presidential election.

Lula was the natural candidate. He had already run as the main left-wing candidate in the three presidential elections held after the end of the dictatorship (1989, 1994, and 1998). In these elections, Lula's candidacy presented a dramatic alternative to existing power structures, in the context of the extreme poverty suffered by about one-third of the Brazilian population. He had therefore been considered unacceptable by the elites, who resorted to intense manipulation of the media to prevent him winning. Despite this effort, Lula almost won in the 1989 election, gaining 47 percent of the valid votes in the second round. In each successive election, he gained more votes in the first round—16 percent in 1989, 22 percent in 1994, and 26 percent in 1998. He was the party's main vote-catcher and this was why he ran in all the elections, even when his chance of winning was very slight. In addition to being a national leader, Lula has always been a diligent and industrious party cadre.

The 2002 election was different: with hindsight, Lula's victory seems pre-ordained (although it did not always feel like that to his supporters at the time). By then, neo-liberalism was clearly suffering a crisis of legitimacy. The metaphor for its fiasco was the energy shortage in 2001, which followed the hasty privatization of a substantial part of Brazil's formidable hydroelectric infrastructure. The shortage affected deeply both the day-to-day life of ordinary Brazilians and economic activity in general. People began to question the neo-liberal model, which had failed to keep many of its promises and had been damaged by the revelations of corruption that accompanied its implementation. Throughout Latin America, the neo-liberal model was collapsing. This enabled the PT, assisted by its "clean" record in local government and its efforts to stamp out political patronage, to gain the confidence of broad sectors of the middle classes. The PT was also known as the most persistent critic of neo-liberal policies, a trait they were often chastised for in the media. It was only natural for the PT to profit from the neo-liberal fiasco in Brazil.

However, the scale of the victory went beyond the most optimistic forecasts. Although the PT elected only three state governors in 2002, and lost the emblematic governorship of Rio Grande do Sul, this election marked the rise of the Workers Party to the rank of Brazil's foremost political party, with more members of Congress (91) and more seats in State Assemblies (147) than any other party; it also became the only party with seats in all twenty-six state assemblies and the Federal District (Brasília). As had happened on several previous occasions, the PT failed to win many key state governorships by a small fraction of votes, including São Paulo, Federal District, and even Rio Grande do Sul. Altogether, PT candidates for state governorships received 21.13 million votes in 2002, compared with 9.56 million votes in 1998 and only 6.7 million votes in 1994. The PT candidates were among the top three in twenty-one of Brazil's twenty-six states, including all the most populous states, such as São Paulo, Minas Gerais, Rio de Janeiro, and Bahia. The swing to the PT in Bahia and some other states traditionally ruled by the landed oligarchy was massive, indicating a marked decline in the system of power based on clientelism and corruption.

THE PT AS AN OPEN POLITICAL SYSTEM

The Workers Party defies definition. It was created by union leaders, in a process similar to the one in which European social democracy was created at the beginning of the twentieth century, but it does not fit any model, not even that of the British Labour Party with which it has some similarities. Margaret Keck, author of the seminal

study of the Workers Party, called her work "the study of an anom-
aly."[1] Unlike the Labour Party, the PT never had formal links with
the trade unions, nor is it funded by them. It is supported by many
Catholic activists, but defends equal rights for homosexuals and is
willing to consider the legalization of abortion. It is a mass party,
operating openly, yet it is structured like a Leninist party, with a
central committee and strict rules about adherence to party decisions
(although, in practice, these rules are often broken). At the same
time, and even more paradoxically, it allows the existence of organized tendencies within the party. Its supporters are active members,
and often leaders, of the many social movements in Brazil. However,
the movements are not affiliated with the party and often clash with
elected PT local authorities. Is the PT some kind of outdated Marxist phenomenon or the precursor of a new kind of political organization?

The PT could be tentatively described as an "open" party, just as
there are "open" works of art to which anyone can contribute. It is,
indeed, a political work of art. When the party was created it welcomed everybody who wished to join. This process is still a central
feature of the PT and explains the paradoxical "PT democracy," in
which opposites coexist, and only rarely do sectarian disputes prevail
over the aims that unify the party. Initially, various left-wing groups
joined the PT with the clear aim of using it for their own purposes,
each hoping to achieve hegemony over the new party. For example,
one of the main groups, Democracia Socialista, which had Trotskyist roots, saw the PT as a transitional organization. Its members
joined the PT but have since maintained their own party structure
and their links with the Fourth International.[2]

None of these groups managed to replace or take control of the
PT, despite intense and sometimes cannibalistic internal struggle.
The sectarian culture was slowly overcome by the way this mass
party operated. However, the "attraction of opposites," as Margaret
Keck called it—the coexistence of different tendencies and schools
of thought within the same party, each one bowing to the decisions
of the majority—is still a hallmark of the PT.

A new contradiction may affect the party following the 2002 election. As it got a massive majority of the votes and elected new
representatives across the country, it reached an electoral density that
does not fit into a party structured around cadres and narrow political groups. This contradiction will appear, for instance, when the
party holds its primary elections: there is no longer any logic to
limiting participation in the primaries to cadres only, as established
by statute.

PT CULTURE: ETHICS AND RADICALISM

To understand this open party, one must know what it is that keeps
the *petistas* together, other than a vague adherence to socialism. It
is not a particular definition of socialism, far less a specific recipe on
how to achieve it, but an ethos or an attitude toward society and
political involvement that combines radicalism, self-denial, and
moral outrage. This is the common denominator of all *petistas*, be
they intellectuals, workers, Catholics, agnostic activists, members of
the MST, or organizers of women's rights groups. An activist within
a particular movement or community who is a radical and does not
act out of self-interest is likely to be a *petista*. This attitude is both
a means of self-identification and an act of defiance against the dominant traits in Brazil's political culture: conciliation, tolerance, and
mutual self-interest.

The *petista* ethos, associated with the party since its creation, has
become the party's indelible trademark. It explains many of the PT's
characteristics, including its inability to act opportunistically, which
was particularly evident in the early stage of its development; its lack
of interest in short-term political gains; and its resistance to political
horse-trading. In the eyes of voters, *petismo* stands for morality in
politics. Many PT adversaries, however, are irritated by what they
see as an arrogant and self-righteous attitude of moral superiority.

Fearing that vague adherence to these values was not enough to
ensure appropriate behavior by members, the first party congress in
1981 approved a code of ethics, making these values obligatory:

The PT is a different kind of party, and it is necessary to develop a new and different set of party ethics, and express it clearly in the statutes. The new party political ethics must be based on four principles: first, the individual attitude of its activists; second, the relationships between activists; third, the concept of party loyalty; and fourth, the relations of the party and its activists with the outside world. By the first principle, we mean individual political integrity, that, for example, does not allow anyone holding office to advance his or her own personal position through political patronage, even though this may be common practice in the bourgeois system. Second, it is essential that activists act in a fraternal way to each other. Third, the concept of party loyalty in the PT has to demonstrate clearly that the party is more than the simple sum of its parts. Fourth, norms for other politicians are not necessarily norms for PT members.[3]

This ethical code caused the party initially to lose political opportunities because of its reluctance, often on moral grounds, to make agreements and alliances. However, as the PT began to elect mayors and state governments, it became more institutionalized and dropped much of this purism. Its grassroots activism lost some of its initial altruism as party cadres were given jobs in local authorities. It was also affected by a few isolated cases of corruption, nepotism, and careerism. Although these cases, dominant in Brazilian political culture, were rare in the PT, they provoked strong internal reactions, in particular among intellectuals.

Social scientists trace the *petista* ethos back to the base Christian communities (CEBs) and other mass-based movements that mushroomed in Brazil in the 1970s. There were hundreds of small organizations, mostly formed by migrants who came to the big cities in the south from the impoverished northeast. At its height, the 80,000 CEBs alone had an estimated membership of 2 million.[4] The migrants had to construct their lives in the cities in very difficult con-

ditions. With little help from the authorities, they had to find ways
to build themselves a shack, get a job, and sort out the other problems of everyday life.

In the past, their needs underpinned populism in Brazil and elsewhere in Latin America. Though not really committed to migrant
families, the typical populist leader gained prestige and electoral
strength by providing the migrants with public services. Brazil in
the 1970s was ruled by the military, which harshly repressed all political activity, including populism. The newcomers could not seek
help from the clandestine left-wing parties, which were nearly destroyed, leaving them with few options. Into this vacuum stepped
the progressive wing of the Catholic Church, encouraged by the
"preferential option for the poor" made by Latin American bishops
at the Medellín Conference in 1968. Some priests and lay leaders of
the liberation theology wing of the church are also PT activists.[5]

With the Church's backing, the migrants could meet to determine
how to satisfy their basic needs, such as providing water to their
community, convincing the council to create a new bus route to
transport them to work, and building more permanent homes. In
this way, they developed the qualities of self-reliance and solidarity
and learned how to take control of their own lives, building their
own identity through the process of organizing themselves. In so
doing, they began to believe that they could challenge the system
that was making their lives so difficult. In the early 1970s, as working
conditions in the big factories temporarily worsened, the influence
of these activists spread to the trade unions, originating a "new unionism." Driven by the same values, new unionism eventually led
to the formation of a new political party, the PT.

The new unionism rejected the official trade union policy by
which the government co-opted or even bribed trade union officials,
known as *pelegos*,[6] to end labor conflicts. In 1974, during a metalworkers congress in São Bernardo, the new unionism launched its
first public manifesto, rejecting *pelego* unionism. The unions controlled by the Communist Party were partly involved in *pelego* un-

ionism, as they had accepted the rules of the game, operating by means of opportunistic zigzags. In sharp contrast, new unionism demanded full union freedom and the right to negotiate collective work contracts. It was also critical of the trade union tax, equivalent to one day's wages per year, which was collected by the Labour Ministry from all employees and distributed to different unions. The tax allowed unions to survive regardless of support from the workforce and encouraged corruption and governmental manipulation of the unions. The leaders of the new unionism were more concerned with the welfare of workers than with ideological debate. Their pragmatism, and a certain disdain they felt toward military repression (which meant that they were not easily intimidated), were other cultural traits that shaped the PT ethos.

THE BIRTH OF THE PT

Among the new union leaders was Luiz Inácio da Silva, known as Lula, a young man from a very poor family that had emigrated to São Paulo from the north-east. Lula immediately stood out because of his ability to organize and unite the workers. In 1977, he led the ABC[7] metalworkers' campaign for increased wages and other benefits. Strikes exploded in the following year, first in São Bernardo and Diadema, and then throughout the state of São Paulo and other regions; a total of 300 factories and 300,000 workers were involved. The strikes of May 1978 broke the military regime's repressive anti-strike laws and expedited the end of the regime.

From the start, the new workers leaders had two key guidelines: first, workers had to be autonomous; and second, strikes, even if successful, would never be enough to push through the reforms required to bring real improvements to the workers positions. In December 1978, at a meeting convened by Lula, 14 activists, including 12 trade union leaders, seriously discussed for the first time the creation of a workers political party. Initially, only four of them approved, but another three trade unionists soon joined them. In

January 1979, the Ninth Metalworkers' Congress, held in Lins in the state of São Paulo, approved a proposal "calling on all Brazilian workers to unite to build a party, the Workers Party."[8]

Events moved quickly. The following month the activists published a "Charter of Principles" in which they said that the problems of Brazilian society would not be overcome without the "decisive participation of workers." Two months later, on May Day, a national holiday in Brazil, they circulated the Workers Party Charter, which stated that "workers emancipation must be achieved by workers themselves." Rejecting the military dictatorship, which was still very much alive, the charter added that "democracy means organised and conscious participation by workers" in politics. In October of the same year, 130 supporters, attending a barbecue in São Bernardo, launched the movement for the Workers Party and elected a provisional national committee. On 10 February 1980, 1,200 people held a public meeting at Sion College in São Paulo and took the first steps toward formally creating the Workers Party. Four months later, in June, driven by a new wave of fiercely repressed strikes in the previous month, which had led to Lula's imprisonment, the activists founded the new party, signing the manifesto and voting in favor of the statutes and the plan of action. Among the signatories were distinguished left-wingers and intellectuals, and the most representative leaders of the new unionism.[9]

The founding manifesto stated that "the Workers Party is born out of the workers desire for political independence. They are tired of serving as electoral fodder for politicians and parties representing the current economic, social and political order. . . . Workers want to organise themselves as an autonomous political force." The manifesto proclaimed that the PT was to be a mass party committed to full democracy exercised directly by the masses. "Participation in elections and parliamentary activities will be subordinated to the objective of organizing the exploited masses and their struggles."[10] From its inception, the heterogeneous group that founded the PT, which included many who had earlier engaged in the armed struggle as well as Marxist groups and theoreticians, chose open democratic political debate, including participation in bourgeois political institutions, rather than revolution.

Thus, with the foundation of the PT, the Brazilian left, particularly those activists still licking their wounds from the failure of the Che Guevara–inspired cycle of armed struggle, opted for exclusively peaceful means for furthering the transition to democracy. The PT provided a political home for the activists who had survived armed struggle and exile, for the families of missing political prisoners, and for various groups of activists and intellectuals who rejected Stalinism, especially the methods of the Brazilian Communist Party, and who had no desire to compromise with the dictatorship. Among the intellectuals and political activists were Mário Pedrosa, Brazil's best-known art critic and a leading Trotskyist theoretician; Antônio Cândido, a famous literary critic; and Paulo Freire, who developed the pedagogy of liberation. These intellectuals and activists rejected the military leadership's offer of a limited political amnesty and a gradual and controlled return to democratic rule, an offer accepted by the Movimento Democrático Brasileiro (MDB), the main opposition party. The ABC strikes clearly made the case for full democracy and social change. The PT was at the heart of this agenda. However, both the two traditional communist parties — the Soviet-line Brazilian Communist Party (Partido Comunista Brasileiro, PCB) and the former pro-Chinese and by now pro-Albanian Communist Party of Brazil (PCdoB) — immediately repudiated the PT's right to speak in the name of workers, and began to contest the new party's sphere of influence.

The new party also provoked important theoretical debates on the left, for it indirectly challenged the idea of compromise so widely accepted in Brazilian society. Until then, few political activists contested the Brazilian Communist Party's view that Brazil was a dual society, in which the rule of a backward rural oligarchy, in alliance with imperialism, was being challenged by a new class of national industrialists. The solution, the PC argued, was to align with the industrialists in order to modernize Brazil. It was a dualist logic that took many forms: modernity versus backwardness; national bour-

geoisie versus imperialism; capitalism versus feudalism. Even before
the emergence of the PT, the dogma had already come under attack
at a theoretical level. In 1962, an influential social scientist, Francisco
de Oliveira, wrote "The Critique of Dualist Reason," an essay that
became the bible for those exasperated with the dualist approach.
Oliveira argued that backwardness was not in conflict with capitalism, but a necessary condition of it. If accepted, his argument destroyed the Communist Party's theoretical justification for the
alliances it forged with modern capitalist groups. In founding the
PT, a party created by and for the very class that the Communists
claimed to be defending, Lula had provided a practical alternative
to the Communist Party's multi-class strategy.

As intellectuals and exiled political leaders began to discuss
Lula's idea of a Workers Party, a split immediately appeared. Most
intellectuals, including Almino Afonso, Labor Minister under
President João Goulart, who was overthrown by the military in
1964, and Francisco Weffort, a political scientist who had written
a highly influential essay on the collapse of populism, agreed that
the 1978 and 1979 strikes had created a new working-class leadership and were decisive in weakening the regime. Weffort also argued that, in a society still marked by an authoritarian culture and
such a profound social imbalance that it was almost the continu-
ation of slavery in disguise, to achieve democracy was equivalent
to staging a revolution. In this way he offered the left the last theoretical argument it needed to get rid of the old Marxist view of
democracy as an instrument of class domination. In his view, democracy was a conquest of great strategic importance for the
working classes and a process, rather than a rigid system, which
has great counter-hegemonic potential. In fact, Weffort translated
into accepted neo-Marxist language what Lula and his fellow
workers instinctively knew.

Nonetheless, many intellectuals objected to the creation of a party
that was class-oriented, arguing instead for a broad-based, democratic, socialist party. In particular, the influential sociologist, Fernando Henrique Cardoso, who had written extensively about

dependent development and who was forced into exile in the 1960s, strongly objected to the idea of such a party, claiming that this was tantamount to reducing social relations to labour relations. He also argued that the new unionists were falling into the trap set by the military government's new electoral law, which hoped to divide the opposition by encouraging a plethora of new parties. Cardoso doubted whether a party led by workers would recruit 10 percent of the members of Congress, which was one of the conditions in the electoral law for the registration of new political parties.

Lula and the union leaders were undeterred. While welcoming into the party members of the opposition in Congress, they reiterated that workers would represent themselves directly in the new party and not be represented by others. Fernando Henrique Cardoso and Almino Afonso withdrew from the project, joining the only left-of-center party permitted during the worst years of military rule, the MDB, later to be re-christened the Party of the Brazilian Democratic Movement (PMDB). Many members of the middle class shared Fernando Henrique Cardoso's view that workers by themselves did not have the knowledge to run a party, far less to govern the country.

However, other important intellectuals, particularly those who had studied the Brazilian working class, joined the party. Among them were Francisco Weffort, economist Paul Singer, historian Marco Aurélio Garcia, philosopher Marilena Chauí, and social scientist Florestan Fernandes. It was an impressive group. Later, after a crisis meeting within the MDB narrowed the options for its left-wing faction, several other members of Congress joined the party. Among them were Irma Passoni, a Catholic activist and one of the founding members of the Cost of Living Movement, which incited thousands into the streets in the 1970s to protest the military's economic policy; the human rights lawyer Ayrton Soares, who had defended political prisoners; and the economist Eduardo Suplicy.

Some progressive intellectuals also rejected the idea of direct democracy inherent in the PT's documents. This idea, which is so difficult to implement in large democracies, reflected the radicalism of the founders of the PT, and, to some extent, their skepticism toward bourgeois political institutions. Obviously, the party entered the electoral game but throughout the twenty years of its existence the PT made mandatory adherence to party decisions. It also imposed a duty on PT parliamentarians to contribute one-third of their salaries—almost a punitive rate—to party coffers. However, these restrictions showed the electorate that the PT was a serious, principled party, different from the rest of Brazil's political parties, which made alliances whenever it suited their personal or group interests.

THE PARTY'S TENDENCIES

The coexistence of different tendencies within the PT was always problematic. This was partly because of the perverse logic involved, in which minority groups systematically joined each other to oppose the majority tendency and thus continually weakened the party, and partly because the consequent exacerbation of internal ideological debates made the party inward-looking, obstructing its dialogue with the masses.

In 1983, the leading group, including trade unionists around Lula, gave in to the reality of the tendencies and decided to become formally a tendency themselves. They called themselves Articulação, and it became the majority tendency within the PT. Articulação was made up of trade union leaders, intellectuals, and members of the old Aliança Libertadora Nacional (ALN), the armed struggle group created by Carlos Marighela, and was led by José Dirceu. Even now Articulação, which conceives of the PT as a mass party, open and democratic, effectively leads the party, sometimes in alliance with one group or another.

Tolerance of the tendencies was shaken in April 1986, when members of another breakaway faction of the Communist Party, the Brazilian Revolutionary Communist Party (PCBR), who were self-proclaimed PT members, were arrested after trying to rob a bank in the state of Bahia. One month later, the PT's Fourth National Conference approved a resolution that made adherence to the party's program and discipline compulsory and banned dual-party membership. The resolution defined the PT as a mass party, not an alliance of political organizations or institutionalized front of the masses (as alleged by some tendencies), which could "be manipulated by any political party."[11]

The National Conference in 1988, which took place while the National Constituent Assembly was drafting a new, democratic constitution (in which the PT and the mass movements played a decisive role), approved strict rules banning tendencies from having their own finances, leaders, and papers. However, these rules were partially relaxed at the party's First Congress in 1991. In 1993, the PT expelled two Trotskyist groups that would not accept these restrictions—Convergência Socialista and Causa Operária.[12]

The fragmentation of the party into a large number of groups was one of the reasons for Lula's defeat in the 1994 presidential elections, although the main factor was undoubtedly the success of the Cardoso government's anti-inflationary strategy known as the Plano Real. Responsibility for the organization of the 1994 campaign was divided between factions, which meant that the campaign lacked unity. In various regions of the country, the tendencies formed different tactical alliances to win a majority position in the PT.[13]

The party also became atomized, as personalist, sectoral, and regional leaders exercised their influence and opposed any form of alliance with other left-of-center parties, which were seen as populist. However, after José Dirceu was elected to the presidency of the party following Lula's electoral defeat in 1994, this resistance was worn down and the moderate tendencies—Democracia Radical, led by federal deputy José Genoíno, and Articulação, led by José Dirceu—became dominant. At the end of the decade, this so-called pragmatic or majority camp elected a third of the delegates to the Second Party Congress in Belo Horizonte in 1999.[14] Nonetheless, the left of the party, gaining support from the deepening economic crisis, remained strong[15] and continued to support radical proposals, such as a moratorium on the foreign debt and the nationalization of the banking system. José Dirceu was elected president of the party for three successive mandates.

Under the influence of Lula and José Dirceu, the 1999 Congress approved a Programme for the Brazilian Democratic Revolution, which proposed a set of structural economic and political reforms within the framework of capitalism to be carried out, not by the PT alone, but by a wide coalition of forces. It was clearly a reformist program, and its approval represented a serious defeat for the left-wing groups. Nonetheless, the left-wing tendencies still have a profound impact on party life. The existence of the Marxist tendencies ensures that the PT continues to be a left-wing party, if not a Marxist one.

THE STRENGTHS AND WEAKNESSES OF THE PT

The PT has been the main political beneficiary of the worsening Brazilian crisis, and especially of the failure of the bourgeois parties, but its progress has been uneven. In its first phase of growth, from its formation until the mid-1990s, civil society always demanded a great deal from the PT, usually more than it was able to deliver. In 1994, the PT went to the polls convinced that it could double its representation in Congress, just as it had in 1990, but to its bitter disappointment it did not achieve this. Nonetheless, it increased the number of its federal deputies from thirty-seven to fifty, and its senators from one to five (see Table 2.1). The party was even more disappointed in the 1998 elections, when it grew at a slower rate (20 percent) to sixty federal deputies and eight senators. This election signaled a temporary weakening of PT hegemony on the left, with the sudden growth of the small Brazilian Socialist Party (PSB). Some PT activists switched their allegiance to the PSB.

In part the PT's failure to realize its full electoral potential was due to its principled, or purist, political stance, which prevented it from making electoral promises it knew it could not deliver, or from using modern techniques of political marketing (although this was

Table 2.1
Congressional Elections

Year	% votes for PT in the Chamber of Deputies	% of PT seats in the Chamber	Number of PT seats	Number of PT Senators
1982	3.5	1.7	8	0
1986	6.9	3.3	16	0
1990	10.2	7.0	37	1
1994	12.8	9.6	50	5
1998	13.2	11.3	60	8
2002	16.5	17.7	91	14

Table 2.2
Lula's Record in the Presidential Elections

Year	1 round: votes	1 round: % of votes	2 round: votes	2 round: % of votes
1989	11,622,000	16.0	31,000,000	44.2
1994	16,802,000	22.0	———	———
1998	21,803,000	26.1	———	———
2002	39,444,000	46.4	57,200,000	61.3

also the result of a scarcity of funds). The orthodox tendencies controlling regional branches of the PT also refused to make alliances with other parties or take other initiatives they considered opportunist. Moreover, the left as a whole continued to be hurt by the electoral system, inherited from the dictatorship, which was deliberately fashioned to favor conservative forces. Under the rules of proportional representation, the state of São Paulo, where the PT is strong, should have 107 seats in the Federal Chamber of Deputies, but it has only 70; in contrast, small states in the north and northeast, where political patronage is common, should have only two or three seats but each has a statutory minimum of seven. Despite this, the PT made some inroads in the northeast, especially Bahia and Pernambuco, states with large populations that industrialized in the late 1990s. The PT also suffered from the rules on party political access to the media during elections, which the conservative majority periodically reformulated in its own favor.

Although PT expanded more slowly than it could have done, its growth was fast enough to leave large organizational and conceptual holes. As a result, the PT suffered significant setbacks and symbolic defeats, even in its home territory, the ABC industrial suburbs. In the second half of the 1990s, the PT gained the support of most state employees, but did not communicate with workers in the huge informal sector of the economy or with the middle classes. At the end of the 1990s, unemployment almost doubled. The PT should have benefited greatly, but it lost power among workers and did not maintain its appeal to young university students, who traditionally have formed a significant proportion of Latin America's political activists but at this period became seduced by neo-liberal ideas. Because of these failures, state employees increased their relative influence within the movement. As they were being hit hard by neo-liberalism at the time, with changes in the labor law and higher rates of unemployment, the PT became caught up in their struggle. It also found it difficult to create a public debate around alternatives, as it was still boycotted by the media. As a result, the PT was unable to react adequately to the big wave of privatizations undertaken by the Cardoso government. It failed to challenge neo-liberal ideas successfully or to formulate policies that would appeal to society as a whole.

Along with neo-liberalism, political patronage, populism, and corruption have remained the PT's main external enemies. Corruption and right-wing populism were responsible for the defeat of the PT candidate for the governorship of Brasília both in 1998 and again in 2002. The PT's main internal weakness continues to be infighting. In the 1998 elections, the PT won the elections for state governor in Acre and Mato Grosso do Sul, as well as in Rio Grande do Sul, but it lost Espírito Santo, the first state it had ever governed, and

Brasília, in both cases largely as a result of internal party struggles. Once again, in 2002, internal bickering largely accounted for the PT's main electoral disappointment—the failure to hold on to Rio Grande do Sul. The exacerbation of internal struggles at a regional level, precisely at the moment when the party was changing from an assortment of factions into a mass party, has been a recurring feature of the party's setbacks.

THE PT IN LOCAL GOVERNMENT

From its first victory in 1982 in the municipal elections in Diadema, a poor region in the ABC industrial belt, the PT began to establish a record of innovative local administrations. It became a trademark of the PT's local administrations to give priority to public health, housing, and education. These policies were often successful, and in Diadema, for instance, the PT was returned to office three times. However, a few of its other early experiments in local power were more problematic. In 1985 Maria Luisa Fontenelle was unexpectedly elected mayor of Fortaleza, the capital of Ceará, giving the PT its first victory in a state capital. As Margaret Keck has shown, the peculiar dynamics of the Brazilian political system made the PT the ideal vehicle for the protest vote, the "last hope for change" for desperate voters. However, the PT administration was not a success. Fontenelle belonged to a Maoist faction within the PT and did not receive the support of the rest of the party. She was also viciously ridiculed by local businessmen and landowners.

In 1988, the PT leapt to national prominence, in particular when the party unexpectedly won the mayoral elections in several large state capitals, including Brazil's largest city, São Paulo, which has over 10 million inhabitants (a third of whom live in precarious conditions in shanty towns) and a chaotic public transport system. However, the São Paulo PT administration was a traumatic experience. The mayor, Luiza Erundina, an energetic social worker, had to fight a variety of boycotts, including one organized by unions and another by the local party branch. She, too, made mistakes.

Despite this, the PT managed to make some real advances. Even so, the experience left a bitter aftertaste for many of those involved, and Erundina eventually left the PT.

In 2000, PT mayors were re-elected in Porto Alegre and Belém and the party's candidates were also successful in São Paulo, Recife, Aracaju, and Goiânia. In coalitions with other parties, it also elected mayors in Belo Horizonte and Macapá. In these elections, it received 11.9 million votes (14.13 percent) and came to power in cities with an aggregate population of 28.8 million people, four times more than it was governing in 1996.

Slowly the PT established a good administrative record, particularly in Santos and in Porto Alegre (see Chapter 5). In Santos, a port with over 1 million inhabitants, the two PT mayors — first Telma de Souza and then David Capistrano — introduced innovative solutions for public health and sanitation problems. They cleaned up the pollution on the beaches and introduced an advanced experiment in psychiatric reform, closing the city's largest asylum and restoring the rights of many mentally ill citizens by returning them to their communities. They also adopted courageous policies to fight AIDS, and repaired the drainage system, built at the beginning of the century to fight yellow fever. By 1992, the PT was in power in four state capitals and fifty medium to large cities, generally inhabited by large numbers of industrial workers. In addition to the city of São Paulo, it governed such important cities in São Paulo state as São José dos Campos, Campinas, Londrina, and Ribeirão Preto, each with about 1 million inhabitants.

After Lula's defeat in 1994, the PT national leadership began to place more value on gaining experience by governing the large number of municipalities under its control and the two states — Federal District (Brasília) and Espírito Santo — where it had elected governors. A special secretariat was created by the national leadership to accompany and help local governments. Slowly but steadily, the PT managed to establish a reputation for honesty, innovation, and commitment to the interests of the population in local and state governments. Honesty emerged as a determining factor in increasing the party's prestige.

Santo André, one of the towns in the ABC industrial belt where Lula began his political career, was the main laboratory for the PT's administrative innovations. The basis of the municipality's plans was the concept of social inclusion. Almost all projects and development plans were directed toward the improvement of the social conditions of the underprivileged and their inclusion in society as active citizens. Specific programs were created for each of the main social problems: a family doctor service to improve the health service, a literacy program for young people and adults, a program for guaranteeing a minimum family income, a bank for providing loans for lower-income groups, a training program for small businessmen, a low-cost housing program, an urbanization program for shanty towns, and so on. The Santo André administration was repeatedly re-elected and won several awards, including Getúlio Vargas Foundation and Ford Foundation prizes, as the country's best municipal administration.

Santo André became an example throughout the country of how a municipal administration could be run on socially responsible lines. The conservative elite was quick to understand the political potential of this image and mayors from other political parties, even some conservative ones, began sporadically to adopt similar policies. At the same time, however, corruption and organized crime also reached new levels as the economic crisis worsened, harming the image of the conservative camp. The problem was particularly damaging when drug trafficking groups were found to have infiltrated high echelons of the state administration, as was the case in Goiás, São Paulo, Rio de Janeiro, Mato Grosso, Espírito Santo, and Alagoas. PT politicians were targeted by criminal gangs, and two mayors, including Celso Daniel, the mayor of Santo André, who would undoubtedly have played a key role in the Lula government, were killed.

In the Amazon region, the PT played an outstanding role in the development of so-called extractive reserves (that is, large protected areas of the tropical forest where only sustainable activities, such as rubber-tapping, are permitted) in Acre in the west of the Amazon basin. The man behind this project was the rubber-tapper leader Chico Mendes, who set up the PT in Xapuri, a small town in the Amazon forest. In December 1988, Chico Mendes was murdered by ranchers, but eventually in 1998 Jorge Viana, who had earlier been a successful PT mayor of the state capital, Rio Branco, was elected governor (and re-elected in 2002, despite his campaign against organized crime provoking fierce opposition). In the Federal District, Brasília, the former Chancellor of the University of Brasília, Cristovam Buarque, who was elected governor in 1994 (and has become Minister of Education in the Lula government), discovered the innovative *bolsa-escola* (school grant) program, first conceived by a PSDB mayor in Campinas, by which a benefit was paid to all families with low incomes who sent their children to school. Cristovam Buarque successfully introduced an expanded version of the program in Brasília. It was adopted, with some modifications, by other local authorities, and then applied on a national scale (though with insufficient resources) by President Fernando Henrique Cardoso.

THE PARLIAMENTARY EXPERIENCE

Although for twenty years the PT had a relatively small number of seats in Congress, it played a decisive role in parliamentary proceedings. Its most important contributions came in the Constituent Assembly in 1988, when it helped block anti-democratic proposals for the new constitution, and then in 1993 when, soon after President Fernando Collor de Mello was forced out of office, it uncovered a huge corruption scam in what became known as the Budget Scandal. The PT federal deputies José Genoíno, Aloízio Mercadante, and Hélio Bicudo, and the senator, Eduardo Suplicy, regularly receive huge votes in the elections. While parliamentary representatives of other parties are often accused of corruption, such a charge is rarely made against the PT, which has strengthened its reputation as an ethical party. PT's federal deputies are routinely found at the top of the newspapers' lists of best representatives in Congress.

Compared with other parties, the PT is still the party with the largest number of elected representatives from the working class and liberal professions. Two-thirds of the party's congressional representatives have links with trade unions or other social movements. The first women ever elected to the Senate were PT candidates: Benedita da Silva, who still lives in a shanty town in Rio de Janeiro, the first black woman in Congress; and Marina da Silva (see profile below), who comes from a family of rubber-tappers in Acre.

PROFILE: MARIA OSMARINA SILVA DE SOUZA

With her gutsy determination and ready smile, Marina, as she is widely known, is a remarkable demonstration of the opportunities that the Partido dos Trabalhadores (PT) has already opened up for excluded Brazilians. Born into a poor family of rubber-tappers in the Amazon state of Acre, she learned to read and write when she was 16 years old and, after a meteoric political career, was elected to an eight-year term as senator in October 1994. Aged thirty-eight, she was the youngest person to be elected senator in the history of Brazil. In October 2002 Marina was re-elected, and later named Minister of the Environment in the Lula government.

Marina's life seems like a fairy tale. In February 1958 she was born in a hut made of the trunks of palm trees and standing on poles to protect it from the seasonal river floods, on an isolated rubber plantation seventy kilometers from Rio Branco, the capital of Acre. The rubber-tappers and their families received little medical assistance because a lengthy river journey separated them from the outside world. Marina's parents had eleven children but, without medical assistance, three died as babies. Marina recalls, "I saw electric light for the first time when I was taken by river to Rio Branco to receive treatment for poisoning caused by a remedy for worms. I still remember the amazement I felt seeing a Christmas tree decorated with fairy lights."

When she was about five, her family moved to the town of Manaus on the Amazon River, where they set up a small store. The shop went bankrupt in five months, and they all traveled by boat, sleeping in hammocks, to the mouth of the river. There they planted cassava to make manioc flour, but again the initiative failed. Marina's father contacted the owner of the rubber plantation back in Acre, and he agreed to pay for the family's return, provided that the family paid off the debt by producing extra rubber. Still just ten years old, Marina used to wake at five in the morning every day of the week, to make the fourteen-kilometer trek through the forest with her father and elder sister, first to slit the trunks of the rubber trees and then to collect the latex. Marina's family eventually paid off the debt. Like other members of her family, Marina was often ill, suffering from five attacks of malaria and two bouts of hepatitis.

When Marina was fifteen years old, two of her sisters died within a fortnight, one from malaria and the other from measles. Six months later her mother died from a stroke. She begged her father to let her go to Rio Branco to realize her dream of becoming a nun. Marina said later. "It was the most important moment of my life. My father said yes and I left the plantation. I first stepped into a school when I was 16 years old."

Despite her late start, Marina proved an excellent student. By the time she was twenty-six, she had graduated in history at the University of Acre, financing her studies by working as a maid. By that time she had given up the idea of being a nun: "I realized that I would have to repress all my sexuality and that wasn't the right option for me," and she married. Largely through her participation in base Christian communities, she became involved in politics. She took part in *empates*, actions of civil resistance, organized by the renowned rubber-tapper, Chico Mendes, during which whole communities of rubber-tappers stopped the tractors sent in by cattle ranchers to clear the forest. She helped Chico Mendes establish a local branch of the Central Única dos Trabalhadores (CUT).

Her husband disapproved of her growing involvement in politics, and eventually they separated. Marina says that it was a difficult decision for her because by then she had two children and was still deeply religious. She eventually married again and had two more children. In 1988, a year after Chico Mendes was murdered by a cattle rancher, Marina was elected to the municipal council. With her dark skin and long, curly black hair, Marina, like so many of the region's other inhabitants, is of mixed ethnic origin, largely Afro-Indian. In 1990, she was elected state deputy, obtaining the largest number of votes ever recorded in Acre.

Marina was very active as a deputy, but in 1991 was taken seriously ill. PT friends helped fly her down to São Paulo, but no doctor could determine what was wrong with her. She recalls, "I felt a strange taste on my tongue, as if I had put a coin in my mouth, I told everyone that I was suffering from metal poisoning, but the medical tests showed nothing." Eventually Marina found a specialist in the field who confirmed her suspicions. The specialist believes that her heavy metal contamination was caused by the strong medicine she received for malaria attacks when she still lived in the forest. She responded to treatment, but has to be very careful what she eats, avoiding all processed foods.

During her eight years as a senator Marina was extremely active and was responsible for numerous initiatives to protect biodiversity and to stop biopiracy. When another *petista*, Jorge Viana, was elected governor of Acre in 1998, she was able to work closely with him to develop, in consultation with non-government organizations (NGOs) and forest dwellers, a series of sustainable development projects, with a US$100 million loan from the Inter-American Development Bank (IDB).

THE PT AND THE MASS MOVEMENTS

Since its inception, the PT has viewed itself not as a conventional political party, but as the nucleus of a network of popular movements. This relationship is strategically important for the PT, because it forms part of its conception of political power. Influenced by Gramsci, it believes in the gradual conquest of political space and the construction of popular hegemony.[16] It was in this spirit that it undertook many important initiatives. In 1981, PT cadres created the CUT in an attempt to gain hegemony in the trade union movement. It also backed a little-known movement for improved health care that had a decisive influence in the creation of the Sistema Único de Saúde (the Universal Health System, SUS), which is Brazil's current public health system. In 1983 it launched the Diretas Já (Direct Elections Now) campaign, which captured the hearts and minds of young people and rapidly became the most important public movement for the restoration of full democracy since the 1964 military coup (even though the right to elect the president by direct vote was only reinstated in 1989, six years later), while simultaneously staging (also in 1989) the most important national strike in more than twenty years.

Meanwhile, the PT's Agriculture Secretariat, headed by José Gomes da Silva, one of the party's prime thinkers, kept the debate about land reform alive, causing this issue to become one of the party's priorities. Some of the leaders of the MST, which was founded in Rio Grande do Sul in 1984 by activists linked to the Catholic Church's Pastoral Land Commission (CPT), were also PT activists. The MST became the most active social movement in Brazil in the late 1990s, when structural unemployment weakened the trade union movement and encouraged unemployed people to join the MST. Most of the participants in the single-issue social movements (which are a feature of Brazilian society) are also active in the PT and the Catholic Church. The PT even has a big presence in more recent movements instigated by the urban middle classes, such as some of the environmental non-governmental organizations (NGOs). It is perhaps not surprising that most of the bills in Congress that are of interest to the mass movements are put forward by the PT.

However, the PT has always found it difficult to transform local grassroots campaigns into successful national movements, despite the success of some protest marches jointly organized by social movements, such as O Grito dos Excluídos (the Cry of the Excluded), led by the Catholic Church every year on 7 September (a national holiday to commemorate the Declaration of Independence from Portugal in 1822). There are various reasons for this: the wish of the local movements to remain autonomous, the PT's culture of not co-opting such movements, and the ability of center and right-wing parties, not constrained by the PT's scruples, to intervene at critical moments. Interestingly, although the PT launched the Diretas Já campaign for direct presidential elections in 1983, it immediately lost control of it to the liberals.

In 1991, two years after being defeated by Collor de Mello in his first attempt to become President (see Table 2.2), Lula set up an informal "parallel government," inspired by the British Labour Party's Shadow Cabinet of the time. This parallel government began to discuss alternative policies and the demands of the mass movement, as well as the country's macroeconomic situation. Out of this emerged Brazil's most important attempt until then to fight hunger, the Emergency Food Program, which associated the fight against hunger with land reform and the redistribution of income in rural areas. This program, which captured the imagination of the country, was led by Herbert de Souza, universally known as Betinho. He was a courageous and charismatic social campaigner and a hemophiliac who later died from AIDS. The government eventually adopted the program, but reduced it to merely a charitable operation involving only the distribution of food.

Immediately after the adoption of the Emergency Food Program, Lula set up the Instituto Cidadania (Citizenship Institute), a kind of NGO dedicated to formulating alternative government policies. Because Lula ran this institute himself, he was able to invite into it the people he wanted, without directly involving the party. With the support of other NGOs, the Citizenship Institute first formulated a policy on housing, aimed at resolving Brazil's serious problem of homelessness, which is considered the most comprehensive study of its kind in Brazil. It then started a project called *Fome Zero*

(Zero Hunger) with the aim of ending hunger in Brazil (a program adopted by the Lula government), before looking at the question of public safety, with a view to tackling the roots of the problem of urban violence. Those involved in the Citizenship Institute, including activists, party workers, trade unionists, and political leaders, are largely party members who are aligned with Lula or people from outside touched by his charisma.

The PT has a National Mass Movements Secretariat and, along with other left-wing parties, it created the National Forum of Democratic and Popular Organizations in an attempt to promote links between the different parts of the social movement and to involve smaller parties within the PT's orbit. The PT's most direct influence has been on the trade union movement, since the CUT, which was created by the PT, has become the dominant trade union force. Several former CUT leaders are now PT Congressional representatives. At the end of the 1990s, unemployment doubled, becoming particularly severe in the trade union organization's main area of influence, São Paulo, causing the CUT's influence to diminish a great deal, while the influence of its main rival, Força Sindical, increased with the support of employers and the government. However, CUT is still strong because it is backed by state employees, industrial workers and, since the beginning of the 1990s, agricultural laborers.

The strongest mass movement at the end of the 1990s, the MST, competes with the PT for political space, despite their intimate relationship and ideological affinities. The MST has a much broader and more ambitious political program than land reform, the issue that led to its creation. It supports the PT in election campaigns and is, in turn, supported by the PT. But it has its own firmly left-wing political program, which originated in Catholic liberation theology (in which the PT also has roots). Activists study Marx and Lenin in Che Guevara schools, and the MST's strongly moralistic program proposes confiscating wealth from the wealthiest, a moratorium on the foreign debt, and changes in patterns of consumption as necessary for a redistribution of income. The PT provides decisive

Table 2.3
Municipal Elections

Year	Number of Mayors	Number of Councillors
1982	2	127
1988	37	1006
1992	54	1100
1996	115	1895
2000	174	2475

Table 2.4
State Elections

Year	Number of Governors	Number of State Deputies
1982	Zero	12
1986	Zero	40
1990	Zero	81
1994	2	92
1998	3	90
2002	3	147

support for land reform and regards this issue as a priority. It has organized several campaigns to protest against violence in rural areas and the assassination of rural leaders, many of them also PT leaders. It does not, however, endorse the MST's political program.

During the 1998 presidential elections, the PT briefly tried to change what had been until then a conventional electoral campaign into a kind of mass social movement, because it was felt that Lula would not be elected without the backing of a strong popular movement, or, if elected with a small majority, would be unable to govern. After Lula's defeat in 1998 (see Tables 2.3 and 2.4), the discussion about links between the PT, the MST, CUT, and other smaller social movements was resumed, with a view to forming a bloc capable of disputing political hegemony with neo-liberalism.

The idea was that a PT presidential candidate would be elected only on the back of a strong, well-organized protest campaign that would be able to channel dissatisfaction, put an end to prejudice, and break with traditional political practice.

However, the deepening of the crisis made this approach unnecessary and even risky. The PT adopted a new strategy, in which it sought to win over the center of the political spectrum and to avoid alienating conservatives. As a result, it decided deliberately to create space between the party and the social movements, opting, for instance, not to participate officially in the second referendum on the foreign debt held by the Catholic Church and a dozen other organizations, although its militants were free to join as individuals. It also got a commitment from the MST not to carry out land occupations during the campaign or carry out any other acts that could be exploited by the right wing to undermine Lula's candidacy. In a controversial decision that alarmed some of its most committed activists, it also formed an alliance with the right-of-center Liberal Party, headed by one of Brazil's richest businessmen, José Alencar.

The PT's coming to power completely changes its relationship with social movements. To some extent, this has always happened at the local level after the PT has won an election, when the PT administration and public employees have agreed to establish relations at a strategic level in which they both see each other as partners in a much broader social and political project. It has been agreed that specific demands, such as a demand by public employees or teachers for a wage increase, must be negotiated with the mutual understanding that resources are limited. This arrangement, however, does not always work satisfactorily, if for no other reason than that in many situations the local union is under the control of a PT faction that is struggling for more power within the party or the municipality structure. Now that the PT has won the national elections, it will face a much larger challenge in dealing with the expectations of popular movements and unions. The idea that relations must be established at a strategic level of interest remains valid, but the scope for problems and potential conflicts is much greater.

THE PROBLEM OF SOCIALISM

Although it has never defined a precise socialist doctrine, the PT claims to be a socialist party and, although it never called itself Marxist, its behavior in some ways is typical of Marxist parties.[17] At its Fifth National Conference in 1987, it began the delicate discussion of what type of socialism the party stood for. It stated that "the conquest of socialism and the construction of a socialist society" are "the main strategic objectives of the Workers Party." Although it did not say at this conference that the party was the only instrument open to workers in their struggle, the PT still used the jargon of an elementary interpretation of Marxism and history to express itself. At its Seventh National Conference in June 1990, it passed a resolution stating that the PT did not believe socialism was possible without democracy: "Either our socialism will be radically democratic or it will not be socialism at all." The discussion continued in 1991 at the party's First Congress, in which left-wing leaders from all of Latin America participated. The Berlin Wall had just fallen. The party recognized that

> the collapse of the regimes in eastern Europe, together with the crisis in the USSR and the other countries in the so-called socialist bloc, does not only represent the twilight of Stalinism and totalitarianism, posing as socialism. In a certain sense, what we are living through is the dismantling of a large part of what the international socialist workers movement has constructed since the Russian Revolution in October 1917. . . . [W]e have to recognize that we are witnessing the end of the cycle of socialist revolutions begun with the Russian Revolution in 1917 and the model of society that they inspired.[18]

However, the PT did not change as quickly as its own analysis required. Despite the growth in its electoral support, the number of its activists declined and many of those that remained were enlisted to help run municipal and state government administrations or to represent the party politically. Moreover, the increase in social exclusion meant that workers with formal employment contracts and state employees—natural supporters of the PT—became part of what could be seen in the Brazilian context as a privileged elite. This made it particularly difficult for the PT to formulate policies that could appeal both to them and the excluded masses. While neo-liberalism attracted middle-class yuppies and others away from the PT, the MST increasingly became a magnet for the excluded and unemployed.

As early as the First Party Congress in 1991, the PT recognized the new factors at play on the world stage, such as the vigor of large-scale capital and the Unites States, the importance of the technological revolution and its potential for changing the nature of industrial work, and the neo-liberal attack on the social gains made by workers over the decades. These factors had brought down further the level of capitalist development in Latin America, a region that, on the eve of a new millennium, was already weighed down by its foreign debt, drug trafficking, and structural unemployment:

> The historic impasse of capitalism in the region and the inability of neo-liberalism and the elites to find solutions means that the left must come up with an emergency development plan . . . and must build an alternative development model based on democratic and libertarian socialist ideas . . . a new economic, legal and ecological order that has as its fundamental demand the democratisation of power.[19]

At the following Congress eight years later, the ideas defended by the various PT tendencies reflected a stronger feeling that socialist ideas had suffered a major defeat at the international level, and even greater perplexity at the increase in structural unemployment and the renewed vigor of capitalism. They also reflected the perception that the party urgently needed to develop a new political discourse directed toward new sectors of the mass population, other than industrial workers and state employees, and a clearer perception of how to make national alliances in order to achieve power.

The destruction in the late 1990s of what was left of the national bourgeoisie by Fernando Henrique Cardoso's neo-liberal policies and its replacement by a new elite, aligned with transnational capital, significantly reduced the range of alliances open to the PT. On the other hand, the pauperization of the middle classes and the general deterioration in the country's social fabric, and even in the material base of the country, especially its forests and its cities, opened up the possibility of a new alliance founded on ethical and ecological, as well as ideological and political, values.

As it turned out, Lula's manifesto for the 2002 campaign, *Carta ao povo brasileiro* (*Letter to the Brazilian People*), was a strong commitment to getting the country growing again and creating jobs, but it fell short of being a new paradigm for sustainable development and was on some points confusingly vague. It also contained a commitment "not to break contracts," which is a euphemism for not declaring a moratorium on foreign and domestic debts, a tactical concession that became necessary in view of the extremely aggressive attitudes adopted by the international banks in their campaign against his candidacy (see chapter 4).

THE STRATEGY THAT LED TO
LULA'S VICTORY

Lula's strategy to win the presidency was composed almost immediately after his defeat in the 1998 election campaign, when he ran only to serve the party, knowing that he did not stand a chance. When asked to consider running again for the fourth time Lula imposed conditions, even before his nomination was official. This time, he said, he was going to be a candidate only if the party gave him a free hand to establish alliances and employ the technical and human resources needed to achieve victory. This time he wanted to win. He was not going to run for the sake of running, or merely to help the PT elect members of Congress and state governors, as he had done in 1998.

In consultation with the party's president, José Dirceu, he composed a strategy to isolate the left wing of the party. They convinced the 1999 Congress to pass a Program for the Brazilian Democratic Revolution, which stated that the revolution would be achieved around three pillars—the social, the democratic, and the national—and that it would be carried out, not by the PT alone, but by a wide coalition of forces. This program paved the way for Lula to formulate his successful strategy for the 2002 presidential campaign. This Congress, in fact, gave Lula carte blanche to form whatever alliance of forces he wished, in order to increase the chances of victory.

As part of this strategy, the party organized a very effective centralized campaign for the 2000 municipal elections. It established national rules, formulated slogans, prepared a coherent "message," and edited campaign materials that allowed it to overcome the internal problems caused by factionalism. Lula was the leader of this campaign, staging mass meetings across the country. Although he was not a candidate, he appeared in all regional and national television broadcasts. As a result, the PT inflicted a major defeat on the conservative political parties, winning a large number of towns in Bahia, Santa Catarina, and Paraná, traditionally strongholds of political patronage.

Following the 2000 landslide, Lula intensified his activities in his Citizenship Institute, from where he began to coordinate a series of working groups on the country's main problems, particularly housing, infrastructure, employment, and agriculture. Long before the start of the electoral campaign, the Institute assembled NGOs and some of the country's leading experts and drew up comprehensive proposals to tackle some of the country's main social problems, such as unemployment, urban violence, and lack of housing. It also organized public meetings with the business community, attended by a leading sugar-cane and alcohol producers' association, and three state governors, and held a round table on poverty with the support of the governor of Bahia, Antônio Carlos Magalhães, the leader of Brazilian conservatives and a symbol of reactionary politics. In effect, Lula was signaling, in particular to the party cadres, that the time had come for a policy of wide alliances and dialogue. The Institute was a particularly suitable base for the move, as it provided a space for debate free from the party's internal power disputes.

However, it was at the insistence of another politician, Senator Suplicy, who also wanted to become the party's presidential candidate, that the party was forced to stage, for the first time in Brazil, primary party elections with the direct voting of all party members, a decision that almost upset Lula's plans. Although Lula was reluctant to compete with another party candidate for nomination, he eventually decided to allow his name to be put forward. Without actually campaigning, Lula achieved with about 70 percent of the votes.

A clear strategy was then composed to win over the center of the political spectrum in the presidential campaign. An analysis of Lula's three previous defeats had shown that Lula and the PT had a captive vote of almost one-third of the electorate, but was also firmly rejected by another third of the electorate. The only way of winning was by getting the support of the one-third of undecided voters who came mainly from the middle classes and the less-educated workers. Thus, Lula and his aides decided, much to the astonishment of the bourgeoisie, to hire the country's leading expert in political propaganda and to form a modern press office. Together, they worked out the best discourse for combating prejudice and raising people's hope for a better future. However, Lula never made specific and unrealistic promises, as a populist politician would have done.

It was Lula's fourth attempt to gain the presidency, and, along with the familiar criticism of the party for being too left wing, critics still attacked Lula for his "lack of formal education," a euphemism for his humble background. It expressed the refusal of the ruling elite to accept that someone from the working class was fit to rule the country. More than ideological resistance to a left-wing party, it was the class factor at work, in a society shaped by nearly 400 years of slavery. The media encouraged these ideas, which echoed the rejection of worker autonomy by left-wing intellectuals, led by Fernando Henrique Cardoso, at around the time of the creation of the PT, and which were nurtured by the low self-esteem of a population long accustomed to being dominated.

The class argument was disguised in various ways in the 2002 campaign, but it was not abandoned. Most of the press, and even some educated social scientists, repeatedly criticized Lula for his alleged lack of knowledge or, more subtly, lack of administrative experience. Lula patiently refuted the arguments and, by waging an extremely competent campaign in which the main slogan was "Brazil must change," showed that the charge of incompetence was completely unfounded. He proved that competence must be political, not technical, and proved to be the only candidate prepared to negotiate a wide social pact to take Brazil out of its crisis. He went so far as to organize round-table discussions with sectors, such as bankers and landowners, that formerly saw him as an enemy to be defeated. Slowly at first but steadily, the argument of incompetence began to work in the opposite direction: instead of fueling prejudice against Lula, as in previous campaigns, it angered people. So his adversaries, in particular the ruling party, the PSDB, tried to exploit people's fear by comparing Brazil's crisis with that of Argentina. Thus, it inevitably became a campaign of those who hoped against those who feared. And, as Lula's slogan asserts, in the end "hope defeated fear."

3

THE MAKING OF A LEADER

Sue Branford

WHEN THE PT was founded in 1980, the freshness of its vision won the support of thousands of young industrial workers who had been raised under the military dictatorship, when left-wing parties were banned. Bombarded by pro-government propaganda on the television and radio, the vast majority of these workers did not define themselves as left-wing, let alone socialist; most of them probably adhered to the practice, widespread at the time, of using the word *comunista* as a routine word of abuse. But they knew what they wanted: better wages, better working conditions, greater political freedom, and the right to reorganize their trade-union movement so that it would truly represent their interests.

Lula quickly emerged as the leader of this new labor movement. Lula is a born leader with a remarkable capacity to captivate an audience. Factory workers will happily stand for half an hour or more, in the hot sun or pouring rain, listening to him. He thinks well on his feet and speaks from the heart, as he explained in an interview in 1994:

> I don't know if it is a weakness or not, but, to speak frankly, I often prefer to rely on my intuition than to work things out in my head. I think that intuition lets you put a bit of your heart in things, and I think to do politics without your heart makes people very hard, very realistic. And I don't think that's good in politics. I don't think that you can be a good politician without deep human feelings, and I don't want to lose that side of me.[1]

Brazil's industrial workers feel an immediate affinity with Lula who, until he became a national figure, lived a life much like their own. He was probably born on 27 October 1945 (the exact date on which he was to be elected President 57 years later) in Caetés in the municipal district of Garanhuns in the poor northeastern state of Pernambuco. His parents were impoverished subsistence peasants and Lula was the seventh of eight children. Shortly after he was born, his father, like thousands of others from the northeast, made the long journey south to the state of São Paulo, in search of work. He got a job in the docks in the port of Santos, loading bags of coffee. The first time Lula remembers seeing his father was when he came back to visit the family, when Lula was five years old.

Back in Pernambuco, Lula's mother, Eurídice Ferreira de Mello, struggled to feed and educate her children. The family often went to bed hungry. Overwhelmed by the effort, Lula's mother decided in December 1952 to leave the northeast and, with her eight children, to join her husband in São Paulo state. The 3,000-km journey on the back of an open lorry took them thirteen days. Initially, the family went to live with the father in Vicente de Carvalho, a poor neighborhood in the seaside resort of Guarujá, near the port of Santos. To boost the family income, Lula, age seven, sold peanuts, tapioca, and oranges in the streets.

But the reunion between Lula's parents did not work out. Like so many other Brazilian men, Lula's father had started living with another woman—in fact, a cousin of his first wife—during the years he was separated from his first family. For a while Lula's father tried to juggle the two families, but in 1956 Eurídice decided she had had enough and moved with her children to São Paulo city. Perhaps because he never knew his father properly, Lula developed a very close and warm relationship with his mother. Even today he refers frequently to his mother's pride and happiness when he finally got his technical diploma, and his regret that she did not live long enough to see him elected President. It is an experience with which many poor Brazilian men and women can identify, in a country with a high level of internal migration and broken marriages.

Once in São Paulo, the entire family lived in a single room behind a bar. They had to share the toilet with the customers. Later, Lula recalled his embarrassment at inviting friends home from school because there was no chair for them to sit on. It was then, he says, that he realized for the first time that his family was poor. At age twelve, Lula got his first full-time job, working in a dry cleaners. After being laid off, he worked various other odd jobs, such as a boot black and an office clerk. He got these jobs in the informal labor market, with none of the benefits guaranteed in labor legislation.

At the age of fourteen, Lula got his first registered job working in a warehouse. Later he found work in an engineering company and, as a result, managed to enroll in a three-year, part-time course to train as a lathe operator. During this period he had an accident on a night shift when he was replacing a nut on a machine while a colleague held down the brake. His colleague nodded off and the blade slipped forward, cutting off Lula's little finger on his left hand; he was eighteen years old at the time. Apart from work, his main interests were girls and soccer. He was a keen supporter of the Corinthians soccer club in São Paulo.

In 1966, Lula started work at Villares, one of the largest engineering firms in the country. In May 1969, he married Maria de Lourdes, a young worker in a textile factory. The following year Maria died while attempting to give birth to their still-born child. She had been suffering from hepatitis, but it had not been diagnosed by the doctors. In 1973, Lula had a brief relationship with a young nurse, Miriam Cordeiro. They had a daughter named Luriam, following the practice common among the Brazilian working class of inventing a new name by combining the father's name with the mother's. The following year Lula married Marisa Letícia, a widow with one son. Marisa and Lula had three children, all boys.

Until this point there had been nothing to distinguish Lula's life from that of thousands of other migrants from the northeast with similar tales of hunger, suffering, and limited social advancement despite years of effort. However, Lula then shot to national prom-

inence as the leader of the massive wave of strikes that swept
through São Paulo's industries in 1978 and 1979 and a founder of
what has become Latin America's most important left-wing political
party. In telling the story, we shall make every effort to use Lula's
own words and those of his colleagues in testimonies recorded by
several authors, particularly the Chilean socialist Marta Harnecker
in her excellent book, *O Sonho era Possível*. Other sources include
Without Fear of Being Happy by Emir Sader and Ken Silverstein and
Lula, O Metalúrgico: Anatomia de uma Liderança by Marco Morel.

*   *   *

According to Lula, his first contact with the union movement came
through his brother, José Ferreira da Silva, known as Friar Chico
because of his monk-like haircut. As a member of the banned Brazilian Communist Party, Lula's brother was active in underground
politics. In 1969, he asked Lula, who was then working at an engineering plant in São Bernardo (an industrial town on the outskirts
of São Paulo), to stand on his slate in the elections for the leadership
of the metalworkers' union of São Bernardo and Diadema. Lula
recalls: "I was a lathe operator, I was earning reasonably well and I
had a girlfriend. I wanted to play soccer, I wanted to go out danc-
ing, I didn't want to know about union matters."

But Lula reluctantly agreed to stand and, once elected, gradually
became more involved in the union, but never followed his brother
into the Communist Party. Though he refused to define himself
ideologically, he became firmly opposed to the existing union leadership, which at that time was in the hands of *pelegos* (conservative
union leaders who worked closely with the employers [see Chapter
2, note 6]). Then, strangely, in 1975 Paulo Vidal, one of the old
guard, asked Lula to stand in the upcoming election for union president. With hindsight, Lula believes he was being used in an internal
power struggle:

> I had never spoken at a union assembly, had never used
> a microphone, so—and this is a supposition—when

Paulo nominated me, I think he was planning to prove—
not just to the leadership, but to all the workers as well—
that he was irreplaceable and that I was a shit and
couldn't get a damn thing done.

If this was Paulo Vidal's hidden agenda, his plan backfired. Lula
was elected with 92 percent of the vote and turned out to be an
efficient and highly effective union leader.

A turning point for Lula came later that same year. His brother,
Friar Chico, was arrested and charged with being a Communist
"subversive." Lula learned of his brother's arrest during a brief lay-
over in the United States on his way back from a conference in
Japan, his first trip abroad. When a lawyer advised Lula to stay in
the United States for a while until the situation cooled down, Lula
is reported to have replied:

Look my friend, I don't speak the language of the people
here, I've got no money, the food stinks, there's no rice,
no beans. I'd rather be arrested in Brazil than stay in this
dump of a country.

According to Lula, the arrest was

the main reason why I lost all my inhibitions. Before, I
had been a typical union leader. I had been afraid of
being arrested. I had been worried about my family. I
had never thought that being a union activist required
very much. But, after my brother was arrested, I lost
my fear.

But several other activists, particularly one of the big names in
Brazilian theater at the time, Lélia Abramo, claim that this account
is somewhat simplistic. As will be discussed later in this chapter,
Lélia Abramo believes that, while Lula may have changed his ideas
about what was demanded of a union leader at this time, it took

longer for him to gain the courage to stand up to the authorities who ruled Brazil for so long without being seriously challenged.

Buoyed by his own militancy, Lula sought to change the way unions operated, improvising as he went along. When he took over, unions were largely apolitical. Workers turned to them for subsidized health treatment and other social benefits, not for real support in their demands for higher wages or better working conditions. The unions came to life only during the annual wage negotiations, and even then the wage increase was often worked out behind closed doors, with little more than symbolic participation from the workers themselves. In keeping with the government's wage policy at the time, there was no direct bargaining between unions and employers; wage increases were set by the government for the whole industry. Lula and the other young union leaders working with him decided that all this must change. They began, however, by making what seemed to be small adjustments:

> Our first big decision was not just to wait for workers to come to union assemblies at the time of our annual wage increase, but for us to seek them out at the factory gates and get them involved in other issues. We knew we had to get the workers to have more trust in us. So do you know what I did? I started to arrange soccer championships: the union leadership against factory teams. Before the matches began, I used to talk to the workers for five minutes. After the game we had a few beers and cooked a barbecue.

The union leaders also tried to make the issues more accessible.

> I noticed that workers used to throw away the bulletin we gave them at the factory gates, when they were 50 yards or so down the road. I realized that they were chucking it away because it had nothing in it that inter-

ested them. So we decided to liven it up, to introduce cartoons, to turn it into an attractive four-page leaflet. The result: the workers didn't throw it away but put it in their pocket to read inside the factory.

In a short time, we managed to create a new awareness. Before, the union building had always been empty, no one took part in anything, but soon all our assemblies were crowded. What was the great advantage in doing this? It was to make the worker feel that the union belonged to him, was a body that would fight for him, go on the offensive for him. For instance, we started doing something that the workers loved—we printed in our journal the names of the line managers who treated them unfairly. In all, I think we achieved in three years things that normally in this country would have taken thirty.

From the beginning, Lula insisted on his own approach. Another union leader, Paulo Skromov, recalls:

Lula had an interesting, if disconcerting, way of doing things. For example, when he was re-elected president of the union, I think it was in January 1978—I remember Lula was still very thin, and wore flares—he invited the São Paulo state governor and the Commander of the Second Army to the ceremony. For us, trade unionists on the left, this was completely nuts, this idea of inviting such authorities. He managed to upset both the right and the left.

In this unconventional way, Lula and the other leaders developed a union movement that in 1978 was able to mount the first serious challenge to the military government. Rejecting the wage increase offered by the government, the metalworkers opted for industrial action. The strike erupted in the Saab–Scania truck company in São Bernardo, spreading rapidly to other multinational companies such as Ford, Mercedes-Benz, Volkswagen, and Chrysler. By the end of the second week, about 80,000 workers were on strike. "It was the first major strike since 1968 and it received enormous support from all over the country," Lula remembers. "In its way our 1978 strike meant for Brazilians what the Gdansk strike meant for the Poles. It was the first time since 1964 that the Brazilian working class had shown such strength."

More than the other strike leaders, Lula was determined not to allow left-wing intellectuals to rush in and take control of the strike movement. He stopped students from joining the pickets outside the factory gates, saying that they should not get directly involved in a workers struggle. It took a long time for him to begin to trust middle-class activists. Even in the 1980s Lula could be heard reciting a phrase made famous by a samba school in Rio, "It's intellectuals who love poverty. What the poor like is luxury."

The left-wing actress, Lélia Abramo, remembers what it was like:

> I wanted to get involved in the strike movement so I went to São Bernardo to see Lula, but he refused to talk to me. He had something against artists, students and intellectuals. But the others — Djalma Bom, Devanir and Jac Bittar — they didn't feel the same way. In the end I managed to be quite useful. As I had been in Europe during the war, I knew how to distribute food parcels. I showed Devanir how to weigh out the rice in 1kg, 2kg bags and so on. He was very grateful. And in this way I got to know Lula. He finally started to talk to me and we became close friends.

The 1978 strike took the government and the car manufacturers completely by surprise. By the end of May, the union had a earned a 24.5 percent pay raise from the manufacturers, much more than they had originally been offered. But according to Lula, the wage increase was not the strike's main achievement:

> The great victory, even more than the wage rise itself, was that we forced the companies to negotiate an agreement directly with the union, without government interference.

Other strikes soon erupted in a number of industries around the country. By the end of the year, over half a million workers were on strike and many earned pay raises above those authorized by the government. The government's wage policy had come under serious threat for the first time.

By the following year, however, the government was better prepared and the unions faced a more difficult struggle. The metalworkers' union in São Bernardo called a general strike for 13 March, demanding a pay increase and improved working conditions. The response was overwhelming. The general assemblies, called by the union, had to be held in the Vila Euclides soccer stadium, the only place capable of holding more than 80,000 people. Lula describes the first assembly:

> When we [the union leaders] arrived, the fences, the stadium, the grass, everywhere was full of people, and the podium was only a little table. The sound system wasn't even big enough for a small room, and I was alone, like a clown, on top of the table. Everyone was getting tense, and the leaders were beginning to argue, because the sound system wasn't any good and who knows what else was wrong. . . . You know what we did? We kept them there for four hours on the field without a sound system. . . . I yelled, the people in front of me repeated what I'd said and it was passed backwards. . . . When it started to rain, a few people started to leave. I shouted that no one there would dissolve in the rain and nobody else went away.

The strike was soon declared illegal, but Lula, showing a new willingness to take on the authorities, told a union assembly, "They can declare the strike illegal, but it is just and legitimate, because its illegality is based on laws that weren't made by us and our representatives." The experience was important for all the new union leaders, as Lula recalls:

> I think that the first big lesson for us was that not one of us, individually, believed that we could do what we did. None of us believed that every blessed day, come sun come rain, we could get 80,000 workers into a soccer stadium. And when we were gathered there, all together, we realized that if we pooled our courage, together we became a giant. Individually, we all had qualms. We thought, 'we can't do this, we can't do that.' But together we did things that individually we thought impossible.

The union leaders were exhilarated by the political forces they had awakened. Paulo Skromov explains:

> It's something that happens rarely in history—that a mass-based movement erupts on the world stage at precisely the right moment, when there are sensitive leaders to take charge of it. At that time we weren't deluding ourselves when we said that we were going to transform the country, that we were creating a force that could free us from exploitation, from oppression. We were doing something of extreme importance. We were making history. There is nothing more exciting, more stimulating for mankind than to dream, and to believe that you can transform that dream into reality.

During the strike Lula discovered his formidable talent for public speaking. Lula, who had never been very keen on reading books, had his own way of preparing his speeches, according to Paulo Skromov:

> Lula is someone who knows how to listen. He used to extract the best things from what he heard and make notes on his hand. He prepared his speeches with five, six or seven notes scribbled on the back of his hand. . . . Lula's speeches captivated people. They were rich in content and extraordinarily rich in form. People listened to him for half an hour and thought he had been speaking for two minutes at most. They wanted more. I remember very well how people looked when they were listening to him. They looked as if they were drinking it all in, savoring every drop.

But there were also difficult moments. "During the 1979 strike, our union was taken over by the police for 15 days," said Lula. "It was the first confrontation we had ever had with armed police, police dogs, firemen."

There was also a time when Lula disappeared from view. The human rights lawyer, Luis Eduardo Greenhalgh, who was deeply involved in the new union movement from the early days, recalls, "The Commander of the Second Army phoned Lula and threatened him, 'You go to the assemblies and you'll be arrested.' Lula, who had never had any contact with the army's brutal counter-insurgency units, ended up staying away from the assemblies."

The other union leaders tried to make up for Lula's absence, recalls Paulo Skromov:

> Djalma Bom—he was the number two in the union— tried to take over Lula's role. But he didn't have the same impact as Lula, he didn't have his charisma. Though the workers trusted all the leaders, they wanted Lula. He had this incredible gift, something very personal. After two days like this, holding assemblies that attracted fewer and

fewer people, we realized that the strike was losing momentum.

Several union leaders, together with Lélia Abramo, discovered
where Lula was hiding and went there. "We went into the house
and found him, dressed in shorts, playing with his children on the
carpet in the living room," explains Paulo Skromov.

Lélia Abramo continues the story:

> David de Moraes said, "We've come here to find out
> what's happened. It would be a good idea for you to go
> to the next assembly." David's understated words would
> have been enough to persuade most people, but Lula
> didn't react. He stayed sitting on the floor, without say-
> ing anything. Then I asked if any other union leader
> wanted to speak. No one did. I'm telling you this not to
> talk about myself, but to tell you how it happened. So I
> said: "Look, Lula, I didn't come here to praise you or
> to complain about you. I came here to tell you that you
> are coming with me to the assembly. I'm going to take
> you there."

Perhaps because she was a woman, Lélia Abramo was able to say
things that Lula wouldn't have accepted from any of the men present. According to Paulo Skromov:

> Lélia was wonderful, incredible. We didn't know what
> to say to Lula, but he listened to her and then turned to
> us and said, "You're right. I reckon I'm wrong. I'll come
> back with you."

Lula adds:

> I had been banned by the authorities. It wasn't easy to
> take over running the strike again. But when I realized

that what I was doing was causing serious problems for the movement, I decided to go back, even if it meant putting my neck on the guillotine.

Lélia Abramo continues:

I took him back. We went into the large room. It was packed. There must have been about 2,000 people there. He walked around the room and then, when he reached the head table, he burst into tears, started to sob. He was cheered. It lasted for at least ten minutes. He recovered himself and made a wonderful speech. For the first time he aligned himself politically with the opposition. He had never done this before.

Even so, the strike was by no means an unqualified success. On 21 March, eight days after the strike began, the labor minister agreed to direct talks between the unions and their employers, but insisted first on an immediate return to work by the strikers. This was overwhelmingly rejected by the strikers, but after heavy intimidation by the military police, many people began to drift back to work. In an effort to limit the damage, Lula accepted the employers' proposal for a forty-five-day truce and a 15 percent wage increase, in exchange for a promise not to carry out reprisal lay-offs of union militants.

Lula's handling of the negotiations was bitterly criticized by many workers and some of his fellow union leaders. He was even jeered in the stadium when he explained his actions. Paulo Skromov describes the situation:

We thought he had made a terrible mistake. Jacó began to cry. I tried to comfort him, but I was feeling much the same myself.

Lula explains that:

Many workers left the stadium that night calling me a traitor, saying that I had sold them down the river, that I had betrayed them. It was a very difficult period for me. Political scientists said that I would never again be able to organize a strike, to regain the confidence of the workers. Paulo Skromov said that I was politically destroyed.

Paulo Skromov continues:

I was having lunch with Lula shortly afterwards, in the union canteen. A worker came up to our table and angrily threw down his union membership card in front of Lula. We looked at Lula. It was fairly tense. But Lula only lowered his head and the worker eventually walked off. Lula turned to us and said, "That's nothing compared to other things I've had to go through since the end of the strike."

But some union leaders supported Lula. Wagner Benevides recalls:

Many workers thought that we could have continued, but it wasn't true. The strike had to stop. Everyone was exhausted. It had reached a critical moment. Lula took the only sensible decision, and his prestige suffered as a result. But Lula recovered. He was born again out of the ashes.

The 1979 strike convinced Lula and other union leaders of the need to create their own political party. They had received minimal support from Congress, even from those who claimed to be part of the opposition, which strengthened their distrust of professional politicians. The engineering companies subsequently reneged on their promise not to carry out reprisal lay-offs, further convincing the union leaders that they needed to take part directly in politics to fight for fairer laws on industrial action. A new phase in Brazilian history was about to begin.

PROFILE: BENEDITA DA SILVA

Benedita da Silva, Brazil's first black senator, remembers as a child delivering laundry to the house of President Juscelino Kubitschek in Leme in Rio de Janeiro. Her mother, a washer-woman, was a *mãe-de-santo,* a priestess in the Afro-Brazilian candomblé religion. "At that time, it wasn't respectable for public figures to be seen consulting a *mãe-de-santo,*" recalls Benedita, "so they came secretly at night." Benedita, one of thirteen children, spent her childhood in a shanty town built on stilts in a flooded area of Rio de Janeiro. Her family was poor and from age six, Benedita worked, first in street markets and then as a maid. "Then I got a job in a smart nursery. I cleaned the bottoms of several leading public figures, whom I now meet as an equal," she laughs.

Benedita married at fifteen, just after her mother's death. By age twenty-two she had five children. Despite the fact that her first husband, a house painter, was a heavy drinker, she stayed with him until his death twenty-two years later. Life was hard for Benedita. In 1968 she could no longer earn enough to support herself and her children. "I belong to the poorest of the poor in Brazilian society," she said. "I'm one of the da Silvas of this life." (In Brazil, da Silva is the commonest working-class surname.) She felt suicidal until a friend took her to the Assembly of God, an evangelical church. The church got her over this difficult period and she has been a devoted follower ever since, even giving up Carnival, which she used to enjoy enormously.

"After the bible, the PT," says Benedita. She was a founding member of the party and has been tremendously active. Throughout her political career, she has turned the triple discrimination that she endured into an electoral asset, using as her slogan, "I am black, a woman and a shanty-town dweller." She was a municipal councillor, then a federal deputy, becoming particularly active in the Constituent Assembly, which in 1987 drafted Brazil's new constitution. She presented ninety-two amendments, twenty-five of which were approved, including the controversial measure to make the job of maid a proper, regulated profession. In 1994, Benedita was elected senator, a position she gave up in 1998 to become vice-governor of the state of Rio de Janeiro in a coalition government. In early 2002, she became governor for the remaining nine months of the administration because the outgoing governor, Antônio Garotinho, decided to stand for the presidency. In 2003, she became Minister of Social Development and Assistance in the Lula government.

Benedita is a vehement defender of Brazil's black population. "The Brazilian nation was forged through the rape of the black population," she says. "Black families were destroyed. My grandparents and great-grandparents were slaves. They had children who were taken away from them and sold. We have no idea what happened to them." Even today, Benedita suffers from discrimination. "I go to the front entrance of apartment blocks and the porters still tell me to go round to the tradesmen's entrance."

Benedita married again in 1982. Her second husband was a northeasterner with a long history of political involvement. In their heated political discussions, he cited Marx and Benedita replied with quotations from the Bible. Her husband died in 1988 and Benedita married again, this time to the famous actor, Antônio Pitanga. Benedita describes her marriage, "I love my husband. I'm over the moon, passion 24 hours a day."

Bendita still lives in the Chapéu Mangueira shanty town in which she raised her children. Like most shanty towns in Rio, it is located on a hillside, forcing visitors to climb up fifty-six steep steps to get to Benedita's house. Though her three-roomed house is much more comfortable than most of the others, she still suffers from periodic police "invasions," water shortages, and electricity blackouts. Some years ago, one of her nephews was killed in a shoot out. After being elected senator, Benedita justified her decision to stay in the shanty town by saying, *Sou favelada, estou senadora*, using the two verbs in Portuguese for "to be," to say that her condition of life was to be a shanty-town dweller, whereas she was only temporarily a senator.

4

THE FERNANDO HENRIQUE CARDOSO
LEGACY

Sue Branford

ON ELECTION NIGHT on 27 October 2002, Lula was interviewed on *Jornal Nacional,* the main news and current affairs program on TV Globo, the country's leading television network. The program carried in considerable detail the reaction of the so-called market to Lula's victory—the small slide in the value of the real on the currency market, the impact on the São Paulo stock market, the view of foreign investors. With a half smile on his face, Lula commented: "Haven't we got something more important to talk about? What about the hunger, the unemployment and the social injustice in the country?" With this observation, Lula was saying indirectly that he intended to change priorities and to place Brazil's social crisis at the heart of policy making. For this reason, his victory was seen as a possible turning point in Latin American history, because it is the first time in thirty years of Latin American history that a President, backed by a large and solid political party, had been elected on the back of a program questioning the central tenet of neo-liberalism, namely that the most important role of government is to create favorable conditions for private investors. But was it really feasible for the PT to be promising this shift in priorities? What kind of legacy had Cardoso left after his eight years in government?

THE CARDOSO YEARS

When Fernando Henrique Cardoso took office on 1 January 1995, he stood for the best of the old elitist civilian governments that ruled Brazil for much of the twentieth century (outside the period of the 1964–1985 military dictatorship). Cardoso was a respected intellectual who spoke four or five languages, was a democrat who opposed the military dictatorship, and was personally honest. Moreover, before entering politics, Cardoso established an international reputation as a left-leaning sociologist who studied "dependent development" in Latin America, and concluded that, far from bringing autonomous development, the close relationship the region developed with the rich, industrialized countries, particularly the United States, had exacerbated social and economic inequalities and increased vulnerability to external shocks. Cardoso argued that Latin America's spineless and cowed "national bourgeoisie" was incapable of using an alliance with "external monopoly capital" to defend its own interests[1] and concluded that the region must forge its own identity and independent path to development.

Because his ideas were considered subversive by the military government, Cardoso was forced into exile in the late 1960s. When he returned in 1978, he decided to enter politics and in 1980 he was one of the founders of the Partido do Movimento Democrático Brasileiro (PMDB), the main opposition party at the time. Having been elected senator in 1982, winning more votes than any other candidate, he helped restore civilian government in 1985 and learned how to operate effectively within the corrupt, clientelistic world of Brazilian politics. By the time he was elected President in 1994, it was evident that he had abandoned most of his radical views: in his desire to defeat Lula and the PT, he formed an alliance with the Liberal Front Party, the stronghold of reactionary landowners and old-style political bosses. Cardoso even stated before television cameras, "Forget everything I have ever written."

Even so, few people expected Cardoso to become a convert to the latest—and particularly vicious—variant of dependent development. By the time Cardoso ended his eight years in government, international capital had taken over huge areas of the Brazilian economy and the country was caught in a foreign and domestic debt trap of unprecedented proportions. Unemployment and crime had reached record levels. One analyst concluded: "The Brazilian case constitutes a laboratory experiment demonstrating how and why the injection of the neo-liberal virus, especially that strain which includes a pegged exchange rate, tends to polarize society and ruin an economy."[2]

THE PLANO REAL

By 1990, Cardoso had been completely converted to neo-liberalism and would have accepted a ministry in the Collor de Melo government, the first administration to apply free market reforms, if he had not been stopped by his politically astute colleague, Mário Covas. After Collor was forced to resign after a huge corruption scandal, Cardoso agreed to become finance minister in the government established by his successor, Itamar Franco. In early 1994, Cardoso announced a radically different kind of anti-inflationary plan, called the *Plano Real*, which was implemented piecemeal and culminated on 1 July 1994, amid much fanfare, with the introduction of a solid new currency, the real, anchored to the U.S. dollar. The plan succeeded in rapidly decreasing inflation to manageable levels. For several years, runaway inflation had been the scourge of the country, reaching 1,158 percent in 1992 and 2,709 percent in 1993. While the massive price increases wreaked havoc on all Brazilian lives, they particularly affected the poor, who were paid in cash and, unlike the middle classes, did not have the protection of index-linked bank accounts. Before converting the price of retail goods to the new currency in the last stage of the plan, the government increased the minimum wage, which is the yardstick for all payments, including pensions, made to the poorer classes. So, in addition to benefiting from the end of inflation, the poor received a real income boost.

With inflation down to manageable levels, it became possible once again to pay for goods in installments in the department stores, allowing the poor to go on a spending spree, buying basic household goods, such as televisions and washing machines, which they had not been able to afford during the years of high inflation. The economy, which after several years of stagnation had already grown by 4.9 percent in 1993 (as foreign capital began to enter the economy as a result of the early round of free market reforms), expanded by an additional 5.9 percent in 1994, as poorer Brazilians joined in the party. The entire country breathed a collective sigh of relief as the nightmare years receded and the population recovered its faith in the future. The PT was caught off balance by the success of the plan, which they did not know whether to praise or condemn. The main beneficiary was Cardoso, widely regarded as the "savior of the nation," and with the backing of the right-wing Liberal Front Party he became the presidential candidate of the ruling party for the elections in October 1994. He won with a comfortable majority in the first round, while Lula suffered his second defeat, not even obtaining enough votes to force a second round.

While it is true that inflation had become so ingrained in Brazilian society that it required shock treatment to break its hold over society, it is also clear that the technocrats who backed the Plano Real (particularly the team that came into power with Finance Minister Pedro Malan on 1 January 1995 at the beginning of the Cardoso government) continued the plan for longer than necessary. Their goal in extending the plan was to use the prestige gained from its success to implement a full-fledged neo-liberal program, which they believed would finally launch Brazil on the road to full economic development. According to Luiz Carlos Bresser-Pereira, a leading Brazilian economist who was Minister of Federal Administration and State Reform during the first Cardoso administration (1995–1998), the team had accepted uncritically the U.S.-sponsored economic doctrine known as the Washington Consensus. Bresser-Pereira sums up the new orthodoxy in the following way:

> The recipe is simple: if a country completes its fiscal adjustment, if it carries out other neo-liberal reforms, and if it opens up the financial sector to the world market, then it will be rewarded by a big influx of foreign capital. Instead of the 'development-with-debt' that characterized the 1970s, it will have 'development-with-foreign savings.'[3]

According to Geisa Maria Rocha, a Brazilian economist who teaches political economy at Rutgers University, the Washington Consensus was sold to Brazil (among other developing countries) as the answer to all its problems. Brazilian leaders were told that "foreign direct investment would perform multiple services to the country: it would help finance balance-of-payments deficits, modernise industrial structures, develop advanced technology, promote productivity and promote the international competitiveness of Brazilians exports."[4] Bresser-Pereira believes that the Consensus was rapidly adopted by most developing countries because it seemed to incur no costs, only benefits.

The most fervent advocate of the Washington Consensus in the Cardoso government was Gustavo Franco, whose familiarity with U.S. economic theory included a doctorate from Harvard University; he became first Director of International Affairs and president at the Central Bank. His enthusiasm infected the president. One commentator said that "Cardoso considered Franco's ideas as a kind of Copernican Revolution."[5] In other words, he believed that they made possible an entirely new—and self-evidently superior—way of viewing the world of international finance. In a newspaper interview in October 1996, Cardoso commented:

> We have achieved something that neither Marx nor Weber nor anyone else imagined—they couldn't have done at the time they lived. Capital has internationalized rapidly and is available in abundance. Some countries can take advantage of this excess of capital, and Brazil is one of them.[6]

Completely won over to the new ideology, Cardoso did not spare his critics, calling them "catastrophists" and "doom-mongers." Cardoso even invented a new term, *neobobo* (neofool), for those Luddites who criticized the neo-liberals and refused to recognize the wonderful opportunities afforded by the globalized world.

In line with neo-liberal thinking, the Cardoso government took measures to change the role of the state, cutting back on public spending and privatizing many large state companies, including some that were perfectly sound. Because controlling inflation was seen as an essential part of the program, it also kept the local currency at a high value with respect to the dollar, enabling imports to remain inexpensive. The government was delighted when in 1998 inflation was lowered to 1.7 percent, less than that of many industrialized countries. The high value of the real meant that Brazilian goods became expensive abroad, thus Brazil began to run a trade deficit (see Table 4.1). However, because there was plenty of foreign capital entering the country, this was not seen as a problem but rather a means of acquiring foreign goods inexpensively.

Not surprisingly, since they had been masterminded in the United States, Brazil's new policies were warmly welcomed abroad. The world economy was suffering from a huge glut of capital, with financial institutions in the rich countries desperately searching for new sources of short-term profit. The decision by many developing countries, under guidance from Washington, to open new opportunities for speculative investment (particularly the hugely lucrative foreign exchange market) came as a godsend. According to the economist Harry Shutt:

> The global volume of business [in the foreign exchange market] rose over tenfold in constant value terms between the early 1980s and the mid-1990s—to a level estimated at no less than US$1,500 billion a day by 1995. Its attraction(s) for investing institutions—particularly commercial banks—are obvious, since it involves dealing in the most liquid of all assets (cash), of which they are bound in any case to hold large quantities and which can be placed in interest-bearing deposits for very short periods.[7]

Table 4.1
Brazil's Balance of Payments (US$ billions)

	1993	1994	1995	1996	1997	1998	1999	2000	2001	2002	2003
Trade (a)											
Exports	38.5	43.5	46.5	47.7	52.9	51.1	48.8	55.0	56.2	51.3*	54.7*
Imports	-25.2	-33.1	-49.8	-53.3	-61.3	-57.7	-49.2	-55.7	-55.5	-42.7*	-41.7*
Balance	**13.3**	10.4	-3.4	-5.5	-8.3	-6.5	-1.2	-0.6	2.6	8.6*	13.0*
Services (b)											
Interest	-8.4	-6.3	-8.1	-9.8	-10.6	-11.9	-15.2	-15.0	-14.8	13.7*	12.7*
Profits and Dividends	-1.9	-2.4	-2.5	-2.4	-5.5	-7.1	-4.0	-3.5	-4.9	n.a.	n.a.
Other	-3.5	-3.4	-3.9	-5.4	-6.3	-7.8	-5.0	-5.5	-6.1	n.a.	n.a.
Balance	**-13.8**	-12.1	-14.5	-17.6	-22.4	-26.9	-24.2	-24.0	-25.8	-23.5	-21.3
Current Account (a-b)	**-0.5**	-1.7	-17.9	-23.1	-30.7	-33.4	-25.4	-24.6	-23.2	-14.9*	-8.6*
Amortization	-9.2	-11.0	-11.0	-14.4	-28.7	-33.5	-49.5	-34.6	-35.2	n.a	n.a
Gross External Debt	145.7	148.2	159.2	179.9	199.9	241.6	241.4	237.9	233.7	223.3	222.6*

*Economist Intelligence Unit predictions

Sources: Banco Central do Brasil, Geisa Maria Rocha, Economist Intelligence Unit, and my calculations.

AWASH WITH FOREIGN CAPITAL

Foreign direct investment poured into Brazil, with the annual net total going from US$3.9 billion in 1995 to US$9.6 billion in 1996, US$17.8 billion in 1997, US$26.3 billion in 1998, US$29.9 billion in 1999, and US$30.5 billion in 2000.[8] According to the United Nations Conference on Trade and Development (UNCTAD), Brazil's stock (that is, the total amount) of foreign direct investment rose from US$42.5 billion (6 percent of GDP) in 1995 to US$197.7 billion (21.6 percent of GDP) in 1999.[9] Not surprisingly, Brazil was fêted around the globe as the latest wonder of the developing world.

While many analysts (particularly on the left) believe that it is harmful for key sectors of the productive economy to be under foreign control (because multinationals do not consider national interests when taking investment decisions), orthodox economists have long argued that foreign direct investment is beneficial for a developing country because it allows a country to have a higher rate of investment and thus to grow more rapidly. This argument makes the common-sense assumption that foreign capital does not replace national savings, but complements it. So did this happen? Did the large influx of foreign investment that Cardoso so strongly promoted lead to a higher rate of investment?

Surprisingly, Luiz Carlos Bresser-Pereira, who was actually a member of the government when these policies were being adopted, discovered that foreign investment had little impact on Brazil's overall rate of investment:

> During the Fernando Henrique Cardoso government foreign direct investments increased extraordinarily: until 1994 the country received at most US$2 billion a year in foreign investments; after the Plano Real the country received on average US$2 billion a month in direct investments. But, contradicting conventional wisdom, the rate of capital formation did not increase and the growth in

per capita income remained at around 1 per cent per capita.[10]

These figures strongly suggest that most of the inflows of foreign capital did not constitute investment in completely new fixed assets, which is what UNCTAD meant by foreign direct investment and which is generally seen as beneficial to the receiving economy. Other uses, it seems, were made of most of the money. Some went on the takeover of existing assets. Indeed, the Brazilian government was at this time encouraging such a trend through its huge privatization program in which state companies were sold to multinationals, often at knock-down prices. The government expected the multinationals to invest heavily in the companies they purchased, but in most cases this did not happen. So the Brazilian people got a raw deal: they handed over control of key sectors of the economy without getting the increase in productive investment (and the influx of sophisticated technology) that was supposed to be their recompense in the quid pro quo. Another part of the money appears to have gone to the lucrative local money market where, as will be discussed in more detail later, the government was paying exorbitantly high interest rates in its desperate need to raise the money to roll over the huge domestic and foreign debts.

Bresser-Pereira points to another complementary "perverse mechanism" at the very heart of the Washington Consensus that added to the harm done by the large influx of foreign capital. It is a simple mechanism that stems not from decisions taken by individual companies, but from the nature of the macroeconomic policy itself in a situation of almost complete trade liberalization. It works as follows: a big influx of foreign capital means that foreign currency becomes more widely available, causing the dollar to depreciate against the local currency. This means that the purchasing power of wages, paid in local currency, increases vis-à-vis the dollar, which in turn leads both to an increase in consumption, particularly of imported goods, and to a concomitant decline in domestic savings by individuals.

This shortfall in domestic savings is covered by foreign capital. The net result is an unchanged rate of capital formation but a worsening trade account resulting from the surge in imports.

Bresser-Pereira concludes that, despite all the promises, Brazil (along with the other countries taken in by the Washington Consensus) gained very little at all from the influx of capital:

> The developing country absorbs foreign savings and acquires great foreign obligations, but it does not increase its capacity to remunerate the foreign investments. The new consensus thus served the interests of commercial and investment banks in the rich countries, which are constantly looking for new profitable outlets for their glut of capital. And it brought great benefits to the governments of the rich countries, as they are always keen to increase their trade surpluses. So it naturally received the support of the two international financial institutions based in Washington: the IMF and the World Bank.[11]

In Brazil's case, the impact on the trade account was dramatic: the country went from routine trade surpluses of around US$10 billion in the early 1990s to heavy deficits of US$3.4 billion in 1995, US$5.5 billion in 1996, US$8.3 billion in 1997, and US$6.5 billion in 1998. The deficit on the current account (that is, the balance left after trade in goods and services, income flows, and current transfers have been taken into account, excluding capital movements) went up from US$1.7 billion in 1994, when Brazil still had a healthy trade balance, to US$17.9 billion in 1995, US$23.1 billion in 1996, US$30.7 billion in 1996, and US$33.4 billion in 1998 (see Table 4.1). Throughout Brazil's history, high current account deficits have usually been a sign that a crisis was approaching, and this was no exception.

The deficits led to a startling increase in the country's foreign vulnerability. Once again, it is easy to see what happened. Brazil needed a large influx of foreign capital (apart from foreign investment) to cover the current account deficits and to accumulate foreign reserves to protect its overvalued currency from attacks by speculators. In order to attract this foreign capital, the government (which borrows in the local currency, the real, on the local money market) had to raise interest rates to one of the highest levels in the world and lay on other attractive enticements for foreigners (such as indexing treasury bonds against the U.S. dollar and authorizing investors to set up bank accounts with free access to floating exchange rates to enable them to move funds in and out of the country at will).[12] In its turn, the high rate of interest led to a ballooning internal debt, which by the end of the Cardoso government had reached over 50 percent of GDP. The foreign debt also grew very quickly (just as it had, in very different circumstances, in the late 1970s), increasing from US$145.7 billion in 1993 to US$241.4 billion in 1999. Even discounting foreign reserves of approximately US$35 billion, this left a net debt of US$206 billion in 1999, which was more than four times that year's exports of US$44.8 billion. The International Monetary Fund (IMF) and the World Bank believe that, in most cases, a ratio of net foreign debt to exports of more than 2:5 leaves an economy extremely vulnerable to external shocks.

As Geisa Maria Rocha has shown, Brazil's susceptibility soon became evident during the Cardoso government. The country no sooner recovered from one shock than it was shaken by another: first, the collapse of the Mexican peso in 1995 and the subsequent aftershocks throughout Latin America; next, the East Asian crisis in early 1997; and then the Russian default in August 1998, followed by the plunge in Wall Street in the autumn. Each time the crisis took the same relentless course—speculators withdrew their "hot money," the government increased interest rates to super-high levels in a desperate attempt to attract the capital back, the Brazilian economy stalled as companies reeled from the high cost of borrowing, recession, and finally the country had a modest recovery.

This chain of events, which has been repeated in so many vulnerable countries in the world over the last decade, does incalculable

damage to the developing nation. Because the debtor country is so
dependent on capital inflows, it is vulnerable to deliberate attacks,
engineered by speculators to increase their earnings. At these moments Brazil's "country risk" (the sanctimonious and self-righteous
term with which speculators justify their exorbitant takings by claiming that they must be rewarded for the high risk they are taking in
lending to an untrustworthy country) rose to over 1,500 points (even
rising to the ludicrous level of 2,500 points at one stage in 2002).
This meant that Brazil had to pay an additional rate of interest,
above the U.S. base rate, of 15 percent (or even 25 percent) a year.
In practice, the banks have rarely paid the price of the additional
risk they claim to be running, for whenever an important debtor
has finally exhausted its reserves and faced default, the IMF has
stepped in with extra cash, always demanding additional sacrifices
from the recipient nation, even though almost all the new money
has gone directly to the foreign banks.[13] This scheme has meant that
for two decades, the governments of debtor countries have been
paying ludicrously high rates of interest and making large contributions to the exorbitant profits made by many foreign banks. This
export of capital from the poorest to the richest nations—which
dwarfs all assistance received by developing countries in aid—is one
of the worst scandals of the present age.

For Brazil, the crisis was most serious in the first half of 1998,
when US$31.2 billion in speculative capital hemorrhaged out of the
country in a few weeks amid rumors that Brazil would follow Russia
into default. Rather than let the real drop to its market level (which
would inevitably happen given the deregulated state of the Brazilian
economy), the government spent half the country's foreign reserves
in just two months in what was to prove a fruitless attempt to maintain the currency at its high level. Politics intervened when the
United States organized an IMF bail-out worth US$41.5 billion to
postpone the collapse of the currency until after Cardoso had been
re-elected in October (defeating Lula in his third attempt). However, market pressure on the real continued after the election. According to Bresser-Pereira, a minister until the end of 1998, Finance

Minister Pedro Malan refused to accept even then that his policy had failed: he revealed that "In January 1999, after a long internal struggle within the government, the President of the Republic, going against the advice of his Finance Minister, decided to let the exchange rate float." If the government had insisted on keeping an overvalued currency until the last possible moment, as happened in neighboring Argentina, Brazil's economic situation would undoubtedly be worse today. Surprisingly, Malan was not removed from office, nor did he resign after this major policy defeat (although the young Turk, Gustavo Franco, lost his job).

Because of the devaluation and the U.S. government's decision to lower interest rates to revive the U.S. stock market, Brazil enjoyed a breather and the economy grew by 4.4 percent in 2000. Yet before the end of the year, the crisis returned in an even more virulent form. The flow of international capital, vital for covering the current account deficit, was halted by the looming default in Argentina and the downturn in the global economy, particularly in the United States. In August 2001, Brazil signed a new US$15-billion deal with the IMF, for which it was required to commit itself to a budget surplus equivalent to at least 3 percent of GDP over the following three years. This time the respite was even shorter. After massive capital flight, Argentina ran out of money to service its US$150-billion foreign debt and, despite desperate efforts, was finally unable to protect its currency, the peso, which in January 2002 broke spectacularly out of the dollar straitjacket, falling to four pesos to the dollar in just a few weeks. Abandoned by the international financial community, Argentina sank into a deep depression, with output falling heavily in 2002.

In 2002, rumors were rife that Brazil would soon be following Argentina down the road to total economic collapse (though this was never realistically in the cards, as Brazil's situation was quite different, particularly after the real had been devalued). In the middle of the year, with opinion polls suggesting that Lula would win the presidential election in October, speculators began to pull money out of the country, saying that they feared that Lula would repudiate the foreign debt and freeze the domestic debt. Goldman Sachs even created a so-called Lula Meter with which it calculated the effect that the fluctuating predictions of a Lula victory had on the real in the currency market and on Brazil's foreign-debt rating in the financial market. As mentioned in chapter one, George Soros, the speculator-cum-philanthropist, even told a Brazilian journalist in New York in June that Brazil faced economic collapse if it elected Lula. He added that "Brazil is condemned by the market to elect Serra [the government's candidate], for in global capitalism only Americans vote, not Brazilians." The comment was seen in Brazil as outrageous interference in the country's internal democratic system, and it probably helped strengthen Lula's ratings in the opinion polls.

In August 2002, the international financial community, which had turned its back on Argentina, decided that a Brazilian default would be too disruptive for the already nervous world financial markets. The Bush administration in particular was keen to bail out First Boston and other U.S. banks, large donors to the Republican Party, just before the mid-term elections. Thus, the IMF agreed to another bail-out, of US$30 billion. In what was clearly intended as a maneuver to gain maximum political leverage for its loan, the IMF arranged for most of the money to be disbursed in February 2003, so that it could first get a commitment from the new president to agree to the IMF's conditions.

THE SOCIAL LEGACY

Just before Cardoso took office in January 1995, he told me in an interview for the BBC that he hoped to be remembered by posterity "as the President who did most to resolve Brazil's serious social crisis." Many Brazilians shared his hope, for their expectations had been aroused by the Plano Real, which, as previously discussed, Cardoso introduced as finance minister during the Itamar Franco government. Because the plan put an end to runaway inflation and increased the minimum wage, it brought real benefits to the poor.[14] The Cardoso government followed up this success by tackling some of the country's most pressing social problems, particularly in the area of public health. It set up an effective program for dealing with HIV and AIDS, based on awareness building and the local production of generic drugs,[15] which means that this illness is now largely under control. It improved pre- and post-natal care, which led to a decrease in infant mortality from 48 deaths per thousand live births in 1994 to 35 deaths per thousand live births in 2000 (which is still quite high, with the rate fluctuating quite heavily between different regions and different social groups). It introduced some educational reforms, including the adoption in some parts of the country of the Bolsa-Escola scheme (by which the government provides a family with a basic income, provided the children attend school regularly). The rate of illiteracy fell from 19 percent in 1991 to 13 percent in 2000.

None of these achievements, however, could compensate for the impact on the country of the government's wholesale acceptance of neo-liberal policies, which meant that, after the initial gain under the Plano Real, no further progress was made in redistributing income from the rich to the poor. As Cardoso accepted the neo-liberal agenda that had dismantled worker rights and increased social inequalities all over the world, some social indicators (along with land concentration) actually worsened during the Cardoso years, despite the improvements mentioned above.[16] The government's only real chance of doing something effective for the poor would have been through strong economic growth, which could have brought some trickle-down benefits. But the specific characteristics of the Washington Consensus, with its strong emphasis on anti-inflationary policies, cutbacks in government spending, and high interest rates, made this impossible. Annual growth averaged just 2.6 percent in the 1990s, which results in an annual per capita rate of growth of just 1.1 percent (see Table 4.2). It was only a small improvement on the rates achieved during the "lost decade" of the 1980s, and it meant that the last period of sustained growth for Brazil was in the 1970s.

Sluggish economic growth meant that it became increasingly dif-

Table 4.2
Average Annual Growth of Gross Domestic Product (GDP)

Period	GDP	Per Capita GDP
1971–1980	8.63%	5.72%
1981–1990	1.57%	–0.37%
1991–2000	2.65%	1.11%

Source: Ipeadata—*www.ipeadata.org.br*

ficult for a worker to find a proper registered job. According to official figures, which are known to underestimate the scale of the problem, unemployment increased from 4.5 million (6.1 percent of the labor force) in December 1994 to 11.5 million (15 percent of the labor force) in December 2000.[17] Unemployment was most prevalent among the young, with half of the unemployed being 25 years old or younger. More surprisingly, perhaps, unemployment rates were higher for workers with four to seven years of schooling than for those with less than one year of schooling. This suggests that, far from helping Brazil to develop more sophisticated industrial sectors that would increase the demand for skilled workers, neo-liberalism pushed Brazil back toward its old role as an undeveloped country whose main comparative advantage on the world market-place was its cheap, unskilled labor. Many of the unemployed tried to eke out a living in the informal market. By 2002, only one-third (24 million) of Brazil's economically active population of 76.5 million people had a registered job, with some form of labor rights. According to Sérgio Mendonça, director of DIEESE, the main trade union statistics department, "The figures show that the informal market is more than saturated."[18] Research shows that by 2002 workers in the informal sector in the city of São Paulo worked an average of 76 hours a week and still earned less than R$240 (about US$80) a month.

Even workers with proper, registered jobs felt the impact of the neo-liberal agenda, as the government came under pressure to "flex-ibilize" the labor force. This was even written into Item 33 of the

Memorandum of Understanding signed with the IMF in 1998, which stated that "though the labour market is not characterised by serious rigidities, determined regulations and labor market policies could contribute to a greater flexibility."[19] However, the government's efforts to water down the labor safeguards written into both the progressive 1988 Constitution and the main body of the country's labor legislation met with fierce resistance from the labor unions. Therefore, Cardoso changed tactics, opting for piecemeal changes, often introduced through the use of his special presidential powers. Among other initiatives, he created the much-hated temporary contract (a short-term contract under which workers are not given standard labor rights), he abolished the constitutional requirement that no worker should work more than 44 hours without receiving overtime payments, and he decided that Brazil should no longer adhere to Convention 158 of the International Labour Organisation (ILO) that places restraints on "unmotivated dismissal."

Not surprisingly, the combination of high unemployment and deteriorating labor conditions led to a decrease in earnings: once inflation is taken into account, the average wage fell by 10.8 percent from the end of 1997 to the end of 2001, even though Brazilian productivity was increasing during this period.[20] By 2001, Brazil had 57 million "poor" people, of whom 25 million (15 percent of the total population) were classified as indigent (a subcategory within the poor of people who do not have a large enough income to cover their basic calorie requirement, even if they spend all of it on food). Possibly because of the rise in unemployment, crime increased: more than 1,700 youngsters aged between 15 and 25 were murdered in 2000, making Brazil one of the most violent countries in the world. Some of the international comparisons are surprising: from January 1998 to December 2001, 467 children met violent deaths in Israel and Palestine as a result of the conflict. During the same period, 3,937 children were shot dead in the city of Rio de Janeiro.[21]

Brazil remains one of the most unjust countries in the world: the richest 1 percent of the population (about 1.7 million people) divide between them 13.3 percent of the national income, a larger share of the cake than goes to the whole of the poorest half of the population (totalling 85 million people). As has been happening in many countries in the world, income distribution has actually been getting worse in Brazil, as the poorest 20 percent received a significantly larger share of national income in 1960 than they did thirty years later (see Table 4.3). This is largely because those with the highest incomes throughout the world today are a relatively small group of speculators, who obtain most of their money not from their large salaries but from hugely lucrative deals on the global money markets. As a result, the share of national income going to wages has declined in many countries throughout the world. In Brazil, it fell from 44 percent of GDP in 1993 to 36 percent by 2000.[22] Extraordinary as it may appear, someone belonging to the rich elite (the 1 percent of extremely wealthy Brazilians) has an income 1,825 times greater than someone belonging to the poorest 10 percent of the population. Latin America is renowned throughout the world for its social inequality and, according to the United Nations Economic Commission for Latin America and the Caribbean (ECLAC), Brazil is the worst of the group as the only country in the region in which income is so concentrated that more than half of the population earns less than half the average wage.[23]

Table 4.3
Brazil's Income Distribution among Economically Active Population

	1960	1979*	1990	1995	1999
Poorest 20%	3.5%	1.9%	2.1%	2.3%	2.3%
Poorest 50%	17.7%	11.9%	11.3%	12.3%	12.6%
Richest 20%	54.3%	64.2%	65.6%	64.2%	63.8%
Richest 10%	39.6%	47.6%	49.1%	47.9%	47.4%
Richest 1%	11.9%	13.4%	14.2%	13.9%	13.3%

*PNAD did not carry out a survey in 1980.

Source: PNAD

PROFILE: JOSÉ GENOÍNO

Born into a poor rural family in the state of Ceará in the northeast, like millions of others, Genoíno migrated to the south of the country in search of work. He became active in left-wing politics in the 1960s and was forced underground by the military, joining an ill-fated attempt by left-wing activists to flee into the Amazon forest to prepare for a rural guerrilla war. The few dozen activists were soon discovered and were crushed in a major army offensive involving 15,000 troops.

Genoíno was one of the few to survive. Badly tortured, he was eventually convicted by a military court. After serving his sentence, he was released and immediately became involved in politics once again. He was one of the founder members of the PT and in November 1982 he was elected federal deputy for the PT on the most radical of platforms.

Genoíno now belongs to the moderate, parliamentary faction of the PT. In 1990 he and Tarso Genro, another original thinker who later became mayor of Porto Alegre, wrote a series of articles, published in the *Folha de S. Paulo,* in which they called for far-reaching changes to the party's reform program. One of the articles demanded an end to what it called "left-wing radicalism," which, the authors claimed, was inflicting a great deal of damage on the entire socialist project. When criticized by some PT factions for betraying his earlier ideals, Genoíno replied, "If I want to reform the world, I have to accept the challenge of being reformed myself."

In 1998, Genoíno was re-elected with a large majority for his fifth term as federal deputy. He became leader of the opposition in Congress and played an extremely important role in organizing opposition to some of Fernando Henrique Cardoso's neo-liberal reforms. He became chairman of the Workers Party in early 2003.

PROSPECTS

For its first six months in office, the Lula government has done little
to suggest that George Soros was wrong in his cynical and provoc-
ative comment that "in global capitalism, only Americans vote, not
Brazilians." His remark was widely interpreted in Brazil as being
indicative of Soros's overbearing megalomania. However, this
misses the point that what Soros meant was that Brazil, with its
present level of external vulnerability, did not have the bargaining
power to impose its own economic decisions on a reluctant international financial community. Soros may have been proved techni-
cally wrong, in that Brazil elected Lula not Serra, but his point
remains apposite, in that, according to his logic, the PT government
can only avoid a catastrophic economic crisis if Lula becomes a Cardoso clone and adopts orthodox economic policies. This is precisely
what Lula has been doing thus far in his government. As discussed
in chapter one, Lula and his ministers, fearful of catapulting Brazil
into a financial catastrophe that could ruin the entire term, have
continued with Cardoso's neo-liberal economic policies. Perhaps
even fearful of their own lack of experience in this area, they have
been even more zealous than the Cardoso government, running a
larger budget surplus than the one agreed with the IMF.

It is true that, within these extremely tight budget constraints,
Lula has shown daring and imagination in his social policies. He
selected some PT veterans, such as Marina da Silva, a passionate
ecologist, to head the environment ministry; Miguel Rossetto, a
known left winger, to be minister of agrarian reform; and Cristovam
Buarque, an innovative thinker and the former PT mayor of Brasília,
to be education minister. But, alongside them, in the heavy-weight
ministries that define macroeconomic policy, he appointed figures
from the world of banking and business who had never been associated with the PT. Luiz Fernando Furlan, a dynamic entrepreneur,
who heads Sadia, Brazil's largest poultry, pork, and beef exporting
firm and is on the board of Amro Bank Brazil, a subsidiary of the
big Dutch multinational bank, became minister of development, in-

dustry, and external trade. Roberto Rodrigues, who has close links with Brazil's modern, export-oriented commercial farmers, became agriculture minister. And, perhaps most remarkably of all, Lula chose as President of the Central Bank Henrique Meirelles, the first Latin American to have headed an international bank (the Bank of Boston).

Not surprisingly, there are enormous political differences between the ministers. Marina da Silva, who worked with the murdered political activist, Chico Mendes, to win land for the rubber-tappers in Acre in the west of the Amazon basin, has never hidden her profound dislike of the intensive farming methods used by Furlan's poultry company. Sadia routinely sends out batches of two-day-old chicks to impoverished contract farmers, who are instructed to inject the birds with growth hormones and to keep them awake twenty-four hours a day so that they eat more and grow more quickly. Marina da Silva, who believes that genetically modified crops should remain banned in Brazil until long-term environmental impact studies have been carried out, also finds herself at odds with Rodrigues, who argues that Brazil will be left behind in the technological race unless it works with the biotechnology multinationals. Rossetto, who is a close ally of the Movimento dos Trabalhadores Rurais Sem Terra (MST), Brazil's powerful landless movement, which believes that the only way to end the poverty in the cities is to carry out a program of radical agrarian reform and take millions of people back to the land to establish new "communities of peasant production" to practice agro-ecologia, a form of environmentally friendly peasant agriculture,[24] has little in common with Rodrigues, who only has time for big, modern capitalist farms and believes any attempt at peasant farming to be a exercise in futility.

Thus far, the radical reformers within the government, with their vastly inadequate budgets, have been swimming against the tide. Their demands have been firmly subordinated to the demands of neo-liberalism. Not surprisingly, this orientation has been warmly welcomed by the international, financial community. Even before Lula took over, the PT's conciliatory rhetoric changed the foreign image of the new PT government. In October 2002, the *Financial Times* published a doom-laden editorial in which it stated:

> All the hallmarks of an impending defeat are visible: a soaring public service debt burden, high short-term interest rates, low growth, a rapidly depreciating currency, and an international loss of confidence. At current market rates, even an optimist would admit Brazil is insolvent.[25]

By mid-November it was tacitly admitting that its earlier judgment might have been hasty:

> There can have been fewer greater surprises this year than the way in which investors have reacted to the presidential election triumph of Luiz Inácio Lula de Silva, the former trades unionist who leads Brazil's left-wing Workers Party.
>
> Only a few months ago many Wall Street analysts predicted that such an outcome would lead to inevitable default by Brazil on a public debt that in net terms amounted to R$885 billion (US$247 billion) — or 63.9 per cent of gross domestic product — at the end of September. . . . But in the weeks immediately before and after Mr Lula da Silva's landslide election triumph on October 27, Brazilian asset prices have rallied strongly.
>
> Since the election Brazil's currency has gained 7 per cent and stock prices have risen by 6 per cent in dollar terms. And last month [October] Brazilian bonds generated a total return of about 23 per cent and were the best performing assets as measured by J.P. Morgan's emerging market bond indices.[26]

As the *Financial Times* suggests, it is now unlikely that Brazil will be forced to default on its debt, at least in the short term. The more competitive real, combined with the sluggish economy that has kept imports low, meant that Brazil's trade balance bounced back into the black to US$2.6 billion in 2001, US$8.6 billion in 2002, and to a predicted US$13.0 billion in 2003. This improved performance has reduced the foreign currency shortfall and, provided it continues to manage the economy prudently, the government should be able to honor its debt commitments of US$23.9 billion in 2003 and US$29.6 billion in 2004. Nonetheless, Brazil faces a long and difficult adjustment process before it can extricate itself from its foreign dependency. According to Finance Minister Antônio Palocci, such is the scale of Brazil's indebtedness, that even with the financial squeeze demanded by the IMF, Brazil is managing to pay just one-third of the interest on its debt and is having to borrow the rest. "At this rate, it is going to take us nine years to stabilize the debt, that is, to get it to stop growing," he commented gloomily.

Throughout the first half of 2003 the international, financial community continued to heap praise on Lula (even though foreign bankers were reluctant to provide Brazil with anything except short-terms loans) and is clearly optimistic that Lula has been tamed. Indeed, there is no shortage of Latin American leaders who were elected to power on a fiery, anti-imperialist rhetoric yet changed their tune once in power, dutifully implementing IMF policies: Carlos Andrés Pérez in Venezuela, Alberto Fujimori in Peru, Carlos Menem in Argentina. Maybe Lula will be no different. Perhaps he has already changed for, as was discussed earlier, he campaigned on a sugary, all-inclusive slogan ('Lula, Peace and Love') that is not indicative of steely determination to take on the international financial community.

Yet there is no doubt that Lula is different from the leaders listed above. It is true he has always sought negotiation and consensus, even in his early days as a militant labor leader when, to the consternation of his comrades, he invited a military commander to a trade union event (see chapter 3). There is little doubt that Lula would prefer to find a consensual solution to the present economic crisis and there is an outside chance that, if circumstances are extremely favorable, the government could create a "virtuous circle" in which interest rates fall steadily, exports grow rapidly, and investment increases, so that within a few years Brazil will be able both to regain a high rate of growth and honor its debt obligations. Yet recent experience suggests that is unlikely. Far more probable is that sooner or later Brazil will be hit by another bout of international financial turbulence, possibly caused by a crisis in another developing country on the other side of the world. One only has to look back at the recent history of Latin America to realize how quickly the international financial community can fall out of love with a country.

If another crisis erupts, foreign banks will undoubtedly try once again to get Brazil to do their bidding. Lula himself is well aware of the risk. In his first post-victory trip abroad to Buenos Aires, he commented in a joint press conference with the Argentine president, Eduardo Duhalde:

> Foreign capital is welcome but, in order to overcome economic crises, we have become too dependent on international financial flows and in this way we have lost our capacity to take independent, sovereign decisions. We have been left at the mercy of speculators, who very often don't even know where our countries are situated geographically.

The mechanism is well known: foreign bankers express "concern" about economic prospects, investors begin to pull money out of the country, the exchange rate rockets, the country's foreign reserves dwindle, default looms, and the government capitulates. As the economist Harry Shutt points out, individual countries do not have the foreign resources to defeat speculators at their own game:

> The sheer scale of the funds involved now [on the world's financial market] dwarfs the volumes of reserves at the disposal of governments and central banks seeking

to intervene in the market in order to stabilize currency values. This means individual states are increasingly powerless to resist any concerted move by speculators (or even an isolated initiative by one of the larger ones) to push down the value of their currencies.[27]

There is an alternative that Soros would not even consider, but Shutt argues for persuasively:[28] the adoption of tough measures, such as capital controls, as both Chile and Malaysia have done successfully in the past. Such a move would be bitterly opposed by the international financial community, but there are precedents. As the influential left-wing Brazilian economist Luiz Gonzaga Belluzo points out,[29] the two largest Asian economies—India and China—both have tight capital controls and showed strong per capita annual growth, of 3.7 percent and 6.4 percent respectively, throughout the 1990s. During the same period, Brazil and Mexico, the two largest Latin American economies, neither of which had capital controls, grew by 1.0 percent and 1.2 percent, respectively.

If a crisis erupted, Lula would be faced with a difficult choice. He has shown during his past as a labor leader that he knows how to fight—and to fight hard—when negotiations fail. His personal commitment to achieving real social change in Brazil cannot be doubted. However, if Lula is to stand up to fight for Brazil's interests, he must have organized support at home. Marcos Arruda, from PACS, a non-governmental organization based in Rio, believes that social movements must be mobilized, stating that:

We need to mobilize to get the authorities to move away from anti-social policies, like those imposed by the IMF. The only way we will get change is through pressure from below, from the landless, the poor, students, workers, the unemployed, the marginalized. The way to open up space for Lula to adopt more progressive policies is to mobilize, so that at home and abroad we can begin to check the power of big capital and institutions like the IMF.[30]

João Pedro Stédile, one of the leaders of the Landless Movement (MST), believes that a similar strategy is required to achieve agrarian reform, suggesting that:

> Under the previous administration, the government was an ally of the latifúndio [landed estate], and the MST and the other social movements had to struggle against both the government and the latifúndio. Now that we have a government that has been elected on a programme of change, the latifúndio will also face the opposition of the government. But this change in the correlation of forces does not lead by itself to agrarian reform. The rhythm and the scale of agrarian reform will be determined by the capacity of social movements to carry on organizing and mobilizing the poor in the countryside so that they struggle for agrarian reform.[31]

Lula's caliber as a president will be judged at moments of crisis. He may, like Cardoso before him, decide that there is no alternative to economic orthodoxy and capitulate to the demands of creditors, even though this condemns Brazil to an apparently endless cycle of underdevelopment. Or he may decide to lead Latin America forward in a search for political and economic autonomy and take on the risks that such a strategy would inevitably entail.

PORTO ALEGRE: PUBLIC POWER
BEYOND THE STATE[1]

Hilary Wainwright

FROM ITS INCEPTION in the early 1980s, the PT has maintained that electoral success is not an end in itself but a springboard for developing radical, participatory forms of democracy that will enable the country to begin redressing the enormous inequalities in Brazilian society. The city in which the PT has made most advances in this sense is Porto Alegre, the capital of the southern state of Rio Grande do Sul, which has been continuously governed by the PT since the charismatic *gaúcho* bank clerk, Olívio Dutra, was first elected mayor in 1989.

Throughout the twenty-one years of military rule (1964–1985) Porto Alegre was a center of resistance. The city's neighborhood associations, which now are at the root of the administration's main innovation, the so-called *orçamento participativo* (participatory budget), provided refuge for persecuted dissidents, and later became an important source of support for the PT. Even before the 1989 election of Dutra, these neighborhood associations (*associações de bairro*) and other urban movements in the city were demanding the democratization of local government, the ending of corruption, and the opening up of budget decision making. In some ways, Porto Alegre is not a typical Brazilian city, for it has always had an unusually high literacy rate, even before the reforms of the 1990s (in 1991 it was 96 percent, well above the Brazilian average of 81 percent). But it has not bucked the Brazilian trend of extreme social inequality: in 1981 one-third of the city's people lived in slum areas. At the same time, fifteen families owned almost all the urban land available for development.

In Porto Alegre, as throughout Brazil, municipal government departments and their leading officials had vested interests in this inequality. Corruption was endemic. The local PT believed that the only chance of achieving change was to open these secretive municipal institutions, particularly their finances, to a process of popular participation. Thus, when the PT gained control of the municipal government, it invited citizens to participate in the decisions about the city's new investments. It calls this sharing of power the *orçamento participativo,* or 'participatory budget' (PB). Through a process of meetings in which they elect delegates, citizens decide on the priorities for the municipal investment budget. They argue for the relative importance of investment in projects of public works, services, and the social economy. The principle of popular participation has spread widely throughout the city's administration. "Participation is addictive," says Betânia Alfonsin, a young urban planner who was formerly in the local leadership of the PT and now works with movements in the *favelas.*

The particular combination in Porto Alegre of well-organized urban movements, strong democratic traditions, and a history of left-of-center governments provided ideal conditions in which to test out the PT's new, still-undefined ideas of participation. Even before 1989, there was pressure from neighborhood movements in the city for greater democracy in finances. In 1985, 300 delegates attended the founding congress of the citywide UAMPA (Union of Residents' Associations) at which time they drafted a proposal for opening the budgetary process. The drafting and submission of this proposal flexed a new kind of muscle that took urban grassroots organizations beyond purely parochial concerns and laid the basis for citywide popular participation. The proposal to open the city's budget in this way greatly contributed to creating the atmosphere in which, when Dutra won office, he was able to discuss with the popular movements of the city themselves how his government should cope with the municipality's financial difficulties. In this way, his administration broke with the previous tradition by which the elected government tied up deals among the political elite. From the start, the PT allowed the ordinary people of Porto Alegre, especially the poorer people, to become a source of power in the government of the city. They became the central dynamic force influencing the decisions of the municipal legislature, in which no single party had a majority.

At first glance, it would seem that conditions in Porto Alegre were uniquely favorable to the emergence of PB, but similar ideas had also taken root in the completely different conditions of Santo André, part of the industrial belt around the city of São Paulo that was the birthplace of the PT and, until the 1990s, was one of the largest car manufacturing centers in the world. There the grassroots democracy of *Central Única dos Trabalhadores* (CUT), the leading left-wing trade union confederation, was fertile ground for ideas of popular participation in financial decision making. CUT was created by industrial workers in the early 1980s to give them independent bargaining strength at a time when the official unions, from the moment of the 1964 military coup onward, "just said yes," in the words of João Avamileno, the city's vice-mayor, a founding member of CUT. For Avamileno, the idea of basing the municipal budget on popular participation followed logically from the way decisions were made over CUT's budget; according to Avamileno, "The workers in each union, through their local and regional assemblies, would discuss and decide their priorities for the whole organization. These participatory methods are essential."

Although the connection between opening the black hole of state finance and stimulating the growth of a popular democratic power was partially anticipated in new thinking in the Workers Party, it was not a fully developed part of its program. From the mid-1980s, as the PT began standing in elections, the party began to debate how to use elected office to achieve the radical transformation for which it was working through social movements. Celso Daniel, an intellectual and activist with a profound commitment to deepening democracy, and later mayor of Santo André, was part of those debates. He explained the thinking that led to PB, stating that "we believed in taking the principles of democracy from social movements, including the trade union movement, with us when we gained office. That meant we had to share political power, the management of the city, with the community." Finance is power, Daniel believed, therefore opening the budget was the best test of the sharing of power.

Daniel believed that these principles, thus far applied only at the municipal and state government levels, have implications for the federal government, something that has gained a new relevance with Lula's victory:

> It's very important to try to build a regionalized central budget, because the differences between regions are huge, so if the President of Brazil becomes committed to the participatory budget process at the central level, this could be very important for the construction of a new kind of federalism in Brazil.

Daniel explained how the present federal system in Brazil is "very tied to the old oligarchies, the old elites in Brazil." Daniel, who was a close Lula adviser, would undoubtedly have held a key position in the PT government had he not been murdered in January 2002; he is one of several PT mayors killed, probably by members of a drug mafia threatened by the new open method of government. He was a prophetic thinker as well as a brave leader.

With the motto "Where Participation Makes Democracy," Porto Alegre, capital city of the relatively wealthy state of Rio Grande do Sul, is a busy industrial, financial, and service center with a population of 1.2 million people and, judging by the crowded bus station, many more who commute into the city from the countryside. It has become an international city not by prostrating itself at the feet of predatory corporations in the hope of inward investment, but, ironically, because it has become internationally renowned for "good government." For political, cultural, and economic reasons, it nurtures this reputation. There are cheap flats especially available for the steady stream of curious visitors.

To my surprise, a polite young man met me at the airport and took me to a municipal car emblazoned with the logo in Portuguese

"Porto Alegre, The City Where Participation Makes Democracy." Before arriving, I had expected to have to hunt down the participatory budget; in fact it had come to greet me. My guide introduced himself as Vinicius. In previous weeks, he had been assisting representatives from the Inter-American Development Bank and the United Nations, and delegations from other Brazilian and international municipalities keen to learn and exchange.

On the way to my first interview, the participatory car paused to pick up Isabella, who was to translate for me. Her father had been a brave senior pilot who opposed the military coup. After refusing to carry out a mission, he was murdered in circumstances that remain mysterious. The memories of the dictatorship and the fight for democracy are still potent. It was formative in the political outlook of many of the activists I met on my tour of the participatory process. Isabella was one of them.

THE BUDGET PLANNING OFFICE (GAPLAN)

We drove first to meet the man at the head of the government's side of the participatory process, the Gabinete de Planejamento (the budget planning committee or GAPLAN, as it is known in the acronym alphabet of PB). I must have imagined a grey-suited, probably grey-haired mandarin, because I was surprised by the friendly, tanned young man, suit-less and tie-less, who greeted me. This was André Passos, a thirty-year-old economist and a PT member since the age of fifteen, now chief of the Budget Planning Department in GAPLAN. His office was full of posters announcing political meetings and seminars. Part of his job is to explain the conclusions of his technical work to the citizen participants, so his political commitment to the process is important. Later in the week I was to observe him reporting back to a 600-strong plenary, answering difficult questions and fielding persistent criticisms at a typically argumentative meeting of the COP (Conselho do Orçamento Participativo), the elected council for the participatory budget.

Legally, André Passos is employed by the mayor, but his job faces both ways. At certain points in the budgetary cycle he explains and persuades on behalf of the government, to the people. At other moments in the cycle he scrutinizes, on behalf of the people, the activities of the government. He coordinates the "technical criteria" for the budget, that is the legal, physical, and financial constraints that it must work within. His technical word is not taken as gospel, however. For example, three years into the process, movements in the *favelas* challenged the government's claim that it had no power to legalize or "regularize" their rights over the land they claimed through squatter's rights. The government had been doing its best to provide sewerage, electricity, and water to the squatters. This was not enough, however, for the tenants who, on the advice of radical non-governmental organizations (NGOs) and law students, successfully demanded that the municipality regularize their living conditions, using yet-unused provisions in the progressive, post-military 1988 constitution. Ten years later, the regularization was completed, carried out under new local legislation, approved to enact the constitutional measure, and considered one of the most progressive laws in Brazil.

André works as a servant of the public. He is powerful but not personally so. Instead his power derives from both the mandate of the mayor and the authority of the participatory process. Over its fifteen years, the PB has opened up a state bureaucracy that is normally hidden. Such openness repels the often corrupt pressures on council departments from private interests. Before PB, such interests regularly short-circuited the democratic process.

There are serious constraints on the scope of the PB, such as the general, countrywide taxation, of which 57–59 percent goes to the federal government, 27–28 percent goes to the state level, and 14 percent remains at the municipal level. There are additional taxes collected by the municipality and they can be changed by municipal laws. At present, or at least up to the new presidency, the trend is toward the municipality increasing its responsibilities (especially concerning new social services) but concentrating revenue from taxation with the federal government—a nifty device that helps central government pay the external and internal debt and leaves social problems in the hands of increasingly constrained municipalities.

The Porto Alegre City Council collects 10–20 percent of its total revenue through local taxes; the rest comes from federal and state grants. Federal law stipulates that 57 percent of the city's local tax revenue must go back to the federal government, and another 27 percent must be spent on health and on education, leaving Porto Alegre with 16 percent of local tax revenue, as well as grants from the federal and state governments. In 1989, nearly 90 percent of the budget went to salaries, leaving few funds (less than 10 percent) for new investments, even in basics, such as sewerage, pavements, new schools, or health centers. Now, 15 percent of the budget each year is spent on new investments.

The City Council is permitted to increase its revenue through municipal enterprises. André stresses the future importance of this, pointing to an information technology company that was originally created to serve public departments and now offers its services more widely. The increased revenue goes back into the company and will enable it to invest in fiber optic technology, which will be a future source of revenue. The city's water company is also municipally owned, and most of Porto Alegre's buses are built by a highly successful company owned by the city council. There is also a growing network of municipally owned but cooperatively run recycling projects. All this occurs at a time when, elsewhere in the world, governments and corporations try to persuade us that "modernization" means "privatization."

Therefore, in André Passos's sparse offices a new local government institution has come into being. It has centralized power over all municipal government departments but its job is to ensure that these departments respond to the priorities set "from below." GAPLAN's role is far more active than simply following up the electoral mandate of one day's voting; it is servicing a year-long process of democratic participation.

CIVIL POWER AND THE
TRANSFORMATIVE VISION
OF PAULO FREIRE

Many of those who theorize about the participative process (most
notably Tarso Genro, the lawyer-philosopher who became mayor
after Olívio Dutra) refer to the emergence of a new source of democratic civil power independent of the state. Genro says that there
are now two focal points of democratic power: one originating from
the vote, and the other from institutions of direct democracy. How
does this new form of power actually work on the ground? How
far does the independence of the participatory process extend so that
it can genuinely act as a source of power over the state? What dif-
ference does it make to the state's responsiveness to the needs of the
people? And how does it avoid privileging only the needs of the
most articulate and well-organized and thus becoming just a new,
more public form of corruption? We attempt to address these questions in this chapter.

It is impossible to understand the participatory methods of the
PT without recognizing the important contribution made by Paulo
Freire's ideas on education. A supporter of the PT until he died in
1997, Freire saw education as a transformative tool that could create
experiences of a truly equal and democratic nature, which people
would then be inspired to reproduce. He observed the way we mock
traditional relationships of power and then reproduce them when
we ourselves gain any kind of power. The goal of his education was
to break this pattern and thus obstruct the reproduction of established power. His emphasis on cultural, as well as political and economic, transformation is echoed in the PT's participative methods
of government. The PT does not simply seek to get into office and
to occupy the driving seat and drive the machinery of state toward
the poor. Rather, it aims, in municipalities like Porto Alegre, to
open up the state machinery and involve all citizens—especially the
poor—in deciding how it should work, forming a collaborative pro-

cess that is both personally and socially transformative. Such transformations need constant cultural nourishment.

The Freire model of education as transformation provides an insight into the paradox of a process, facilitated by the government, which produces a form of citizens' power that is a democratic check on the apparatus of the state. PB is coordinated by the local government, just as a Freirian teacher coordinates the education process; in both cases frameworks are open to change and in both cases it is assumed that citizens have their own demands, organization, and knowledge. Thus, just as the teacher assumes that students already have knowledge and treats education as a collaboration, the PT's political understanding was always that it would share with the community whatever power it gained through electoral success, and would be open to their knowledge as well.

THE OFFICE FOR COORDINATING
RELATIONS WITH THE COMMUNITY

We drove next through the port area of the city to a converted bus depot, where the offices of the Coordenação de Relações com as Comunidades (Coordination Committee for Relations with the Community, or CRC) are located. This is where the influence of Freire's fusion of education and political transformation was most evident. After walking through a series of somewhat chaotic offices, reminiscent of a leaflet warehouse, we reached Assis Brasil, the jovial and universally flirtatious head of CRC, who invited us to sit down and talk with him and some of the regional PB coordinators.

There are twenty coordinators, one for each region of the city and four working on particular themes: women, youth, black people, and older people. Assis introduced me to those who were hanging around the office, picking up leaflets. Some of the people we met had been priests. The influence of radical Catholicism is pervasive amongst the PT and its supporters. Some members, especially female members, had trained to join a religious order as a way of

gaining education and getting out of the *favelas*, but left before taking their final vows. Others were active in the neighborhood movements, fighting for the legalization of squatted land or for sewage
or rubbish collection. Several other members had been active in the
landless movement before coming to the city, and a few were committed intellectuals, teachers, and academics.

In the first fifteen years of the PT's administration, the CRC has
played a crucial role in organizing PB. The CRC coordinators' most
important role is working with the PB delegates elected by the first
regional PB plenaries. In practice, the PB coordinators help the PB
delegates with three tasks. First, there are the discussions with technical people from the town hall regarding the practicalities of different improvements; second, there are neighborhood meetings to
develop proposals and hear people's views on them; and third, there
is the establishment of a hierarchy of priorities to put to their region's second plenary and from there to the budgetary council.
These three tasks are the responsibility of the delegates and the community. Although local government does not co-manage this part
of the process, the coordinators have the responsibility of ensuring
that people have access to technical information and of helping
groups to communicate with each other. This enables delegates,
who have to choose between competing priorities, to understand
the needs of the region as a whole. In one region, Restinga, they
had nearly fifty community meetings during this vital intermediary
period before arriving at their priorities. "Coordinators vary," said
Luciano Brunet. In the 1970s, Brunet was part of the student movement resisting the dictatorship before he and his strong feminist
partner, Helene, became founding members of the PT; today he
works closely with Assis. "Their role depends a lot on how strong
and confident the local organizations are. Some coordinators encourage the community to be really innovative," explains Brunet. At
one stage, there were complaints of coordinators becoming too involved and undermining the independence of the local organizations. "Because of this," explains Luciano, "there's an unwritten rule
that regional coordinators do not live in the region where they work

or, if they do, they are not personally involved in the local organizations."

The more Luciano explained the inner realities of the CRC and the work of the coordinators, the more it seemed that, while André's department was the technical engine-room of PB, the CRC was its social and political fuel injection system. The vital role of the PB coordinators in Porto Alegre contrasts starkly with recent U.S. experience, in which local authorities, under national pressure, have cut to the point of elimination their community development and adult education programs. The Brazilian example contains salutary lessons for any strategy of real community involvement. In Porto Alegre, genuine citizen participation in decision making is taken seriously. The work of PB coordinators is crucial to the development of people's power to control the local state. They have to be extremely skilled, exerting authority with government departments, while at the same time teaching ordinary people to develop their own power and capacity to organize.

MAPPING THE WHOLE PROCESS

After an afternoon with the government's budget committee and the following morning with community coordinators, I began to get a clearer grasp of the whole process. The mechanisms of the PB are clear, though complex and original. There is a cycle of three types of PB meetings annually — regional and thematic plenaries, forums of regional delegates, and the budget council (the COP). The first round of plenary meetings, held in each of the sixteen regions of the city, takes place in March. These plenaries focus on the previous year's spending. Government officials, flanked by citizens' delegates, explain the timing and quality of the delivery of the actions agreed by the neighborhood the year before to determine if everything has gone according to the plan. This first plenary in the year also elects regional delegates for the next stage in the process: the delegates' forums, at which each region will establish its priorities.[2] This is where the CRC's PB coordinators' work can be vital. In addition, this first plenary elects two city delegates to be members of the COP.

Before the regional delegates make decisions about regional priorities, they meet with their groups to seek out their views on areas, such as road building, schools, health provision, sewerage, economic development including cooperatives, and leisure and sports facilities. The regional delegates meet together monthly, or more often, to work out the proposed priorities for the region. The delegates then gather at the delegates' forum, where they work out budget priorities for their region by combining two objective criteria (population size and statistically measured need) with one subjective criterion (the priority given to different issues by the community). They apply a weighting system so that quantitative weights can be given to different areas of investment. The same criteria are applied across the city. This weighting system, sometimes known as the "budget matrix," plays a crucial role in creating awareness of the needs of both the different regions and the city as a whole.

The municipal government also holds plenaries around themes, bringing together people from across the city with a common interest, such as education, health, culture, and economics. These important thematic plenaries also elect delegates to the COP, which begins meeting in July or August. The COP is a powerful body that negotiates the final investment priorities for the city, on the basis of input from the regions and the thematic groups. In addition, it considers some projects proposed by the government itself. Through an open process of negotiation and reporting back, the COP drafts the overall budget and presents it to the mayor and municipal council for final agreement.

PEOPLE'S PLENARIES:
ACCOUNTABILITY AND VISION

I was able to see this co-management in action at a plenary on my second evening in Porto Alegre. It was the opening meeting of the 2001 budgetary process in the Northern zone. Our taxi sped northward, over smooth roads, past numerous construction projects. Isabella and I were dropped off behind a fleet of minibuses in sight of a long queue to the entrance of the building where the meeting was to be held. The CRC's budget coordinators provided the minibuses for people with no transport. As people entered the meeting, they registered their name, address, and the name of their association, even if it was only an informal street organization they were part of.

Registration is important for several reasons. First, it counts the number of people at the meeting, which today is the basis on which participants elect their delegates. At first, a very simple method was used: one delegate per five people at the meeting, then one per ten, then one per twenty, as involvement in PB meetings grew (from 1,000 in 1990, to 3,700 in 1991, to 10,000 in 1993, to 20,000 in 1997, and in 2003 to around 40,000). But finally, in 1997, the COP had to change the rules to make sure that all areas of the city are represented, even areas where people are not very active. Now meetings with an attendance of up to one hundred choose one delegate for every ten people, meetings with an attendance of 101 to 1,000 choose one for every seventy, and meetings of more than 1,000 choose one for every eighty.

The school that hosted the assembly provided the entire ground floor for registration but it still took time. While people waited, a troupe of actors put on a kind of street theater, focusing on local problems. To an outsider, the people streaming in seemed to be a cross-section of the whole of the community: white-haired matrons; eager schoolgirls; young rastafarian men; the anxious poor, often black; glamorous young student types with a tan; confident-looking middle-aged men of various shades of brown. But the coordinators explained that some neighborhoods were much better represented than others and this was another reason for the registration, for it enabled them to identify areas, or groups of people, that were not well represented and find out why. Around 600 people had come, out of a community of 3,000. The majority attending that night were women.

If the structure of the cycle of meetings is PB's blueprint, it is the participants themselves who give it life. During meetings there is an opportunity not only to protest and let off steam, but also to explore needs and propose solutions. A statistical survey of the participation of different social groups by CIDADE, an independent research organization, shows that a large majority of the participants are unskilled workers with only a primary level of education. Women, too, are very well represented: over the last four years there have been more women than men at the plenaries, and more women than men have been elected delegates. This is impressive for a region that is renowned throughout Brazil for its machismo. Additionally, in a city that until recently excluded black people from the main supermarkets and factory jobs, it is particularly noteworthy that at least one-quarter of the delegates to the COP are black or indigenous people. PB meetings have become a focal point for people previously excluded from the political process.

The people crowding into the vast school hall saw the meeting as an opportunity to vent their feelings to government representatives, as well as to win over their neighbors in support of their chosen causes. A local tradition of public story-telling makes for a hall full of vivid narrators of tales of municipal failings (two groups were particularly vociferous). In the previous year's budget, sanitation had been a high priority but, complained speaker after speaker, the problems of dirty water and open sewers remained, despite the large sums of money spent on the area. People from one neighborhood complained about a stream that had become the local sewer, saying that they wanted it closed over so it could not be used in this way. Government officials at the meeting said that, for environmental reasons, the stream should remain a stream but they promised to clean it. Another vocal group was from a local school. They had come to a budget plenary for the first time and used it simply to shout out their complaints. The Mayor, Raoul Pont, responded, urging them to elect a delegate, turn their complaints into proposals, and negotiate for funds through PB.

On the platform at the front of the hall sat a mixture of people, some from the municipality's executive departments, some from the community. Beside the mayor was André Passos, next to him Luciano from the CRC; from the community there were the current delegates to the COP from this region, as well as two *vereadores* (the elected members of the municipal legislative assembly for the area). Once the long queue of people registering had snaked its way into the hall and we were settling down in our seats, the chair asked for an indication of how many were attending their first PB meeting. Over 300 hands went up. This is quite common; new people are constantly engaging in the process. Despite hostile local media, recent surveys show that over 85 percent of Porto Alegrans know about and support PB. They find out about it through their neighbors and friends, through leaflets, and through delegates, like the ones they were about to elect at this meeting. PB itself has become a form of media.

Later in my visit I discussed these plenaries with Eduardo Utzig, who, as a social researcher and a former senior government official (when Tarso Genro was mayor), has a comprehensive and reflective understanding of the process. He said that the PB's influence has grown. "The people notice if works are late and the delegates put pressure on the government, 'Why is there a delay?' they ask. And, if the problem isn't solved, they mobilise the community and bring them into the city hall," Utzig explained. Utzig certainly felt he had been under constant direct popular pressure when he was in government, and he thought this made him more efficient. He said that the pressure does not come in a form that officials can easily control because there is no single formal procedure. It can be direct to government departments, to the mayor, through the budget council, or through the regional PB coordinators.

The rules and criteria for PB are mathematically precise and treated with great seriousness by government and community alike. Rules for the participatory budgeting process are written up as a handbook, called *Procedures of the Participatory Budget*, which is annually revised, reflecting the continuing process of refinement and adaptation. All of the approximately 600 people attending a plenary meeting have a copy. Thus PB is a self-reproducing and self-regulating process, with formalized mechanisms for learning, monitoring, and adapting.

THE PEOPLE'S DELEGATES

The main role of the delegates elected at the first plenaries is to sound people out and to listen. Delegates bring the result of these visits to regular meetings for preparing the region's priorities. They also meet together throughout the year to iron out problems, monitor progress, and encourage ideas for next year's budget. They keep in regular touch with the region's two representatives on the COP. These COP representatives are accountable to the regional delegates and could in theory be recalled by a specially convened plenary, though this has yet to happen. This notion of recall, or *retorno*, is an important one in the participatory process, demonstrating the accountability of representatives on the powerful budget council, the apex of the entire process.

Delegates at both the regional and the city level are regularly under pressure from their electors, according to Jussara Bechstein-Silva (hybrid German–Brazilian names are common in a city that was host to large migrations from Europe in the late nineteenth century, especially from Germany and Italy), who represents the central region on the COP. She is a forceful charismatic leader in Vila Planetário, fighting for the land to be regularized and its present residents to remain in the center of the city. She found it hard being a COP representative, explaining that "you have to answer to the local inhabitants who are asking: 'Why is it so delayed? Why is it failing?' And you have to answer to the council too. You are pressured on both sides." But she felt supported, stating that "the mayor, Olívio Dutra, came one night in the pouring rain and told us to be hopeful because the construction would be completed. And we had a lot of support from our lawyer" (a woman who worked in the planning department, part of whose job was to provide technical support for the community).

The openness of the election of delegates can be hijacked. In one region, the system was manipulated by a private company, who paid people to attend the plenary and to elect delegates supportive of their business interests. The other delegates realized what was happening and the ensuing conflicts ended in the police station. The longer-term result was a system of very tough rules to guard against such abuse. For example, any delegate who misses more than three meetings has to be replaced, which minimizes the extent to which people get elected simply to lobby for a single project.

THE BUDGET COUNCIL (COP)

Finally, all that remained to be visited was the COP itself. In most modern societies, important meetings are closed or, if they are formally open, they are in practice surrounded by so much red tape that they might as well be closed. But in the *petista* version of Brazilian culture, it seems everything is open (just about: there must be some closed doors somewhere). So, along with at least two other international visitors, Isabella and I sat in on a COP meeting. It was held in the same rather nondescript municipal building in which André Passos had his office. There were about twenty city delegates there (a full attendance would be over forty delegates) with only two members of the government. It is revealing that, though the majority of people who attend the open plenaries are women, the majority of the approximately twenty COP delegates attending this meeting were men. Two were black, most were mixed race, and there was one deaf man and his signer. At the desk in front sat André, Assis, and two community representatives, one of whom took the chair.

By April, preparation of the budget proposal and the Investment Plan is complete. Proposals are submitted to the municipal assembly in December and agreed by the mayor the next February. So the meeting we attended in June dealt with concerns outside the main priorities. Discussion focused on a sports hall here, some cultural activity there. There were some complaints and some questions.

Even though the agenda was not as important as at some meetings, it was a rumbustious affair. André and Assis, as government representatives, were put on the spot mercilessly. At one point, halfway through a hot and grueling meeting, they were both out of the room. Delegates suspected a caucus of the two officials and, to retrieve their position, Assis bounced back by joking, "Can't a man have a piss?"

Betânia Alfonsin, the urban planner who works closely with neighborhood groups in areas such as Vila Planetário and has a long experience of the PB, said she had been impressed by the COP meetings. "I was surprised. I felt these people are doing far more for the city than we do in our departments," she explained. And they are doing it unpaid. Even though COP meetings take place for two hours every week, all year round (except February), and twice a week in the period from September until November (when the investment plan is decided), delegates receive no payment whatsoever. "The whole system of the participatory budget runs off militancy," explains Valério Lopes, the president of the financial committee of UAMPA, the city's network of neighborhood associations. "The only people who receive payment are the municipal workers related to the process. The delegates have to take care of all their expenses, including bus tickets or petrol."

The overall budget for 2001 was R$600 million (about US$230 million), of which R$90 million was available for new investments, to be decided through PB, then ratified by the mayor and finally proposed to the municipal legislature (*Câmara de Vereadores*). At this point André Passos and his colleagues can introduce into the discussion government proposals that target the entire city and have not been through the PB system. One popular City Congress proposal was the redevelopment of the closed market into an attractive multi-use public center. Such proposals do not automatically get accepted now, though they used to in the early days. "People didn't have the information the government had and they weren't able to discuss on equal terms," commented Sérgio Baerlie, a long-time observer of the process. He drew an important conclusion, explaining that "sometimes it's not enough to have the opportunity to decide, if you don't have the instruments—such as the information and consciousness—to debate on equal terms." Delegates debate on more equal terms now than they did at first. "People don't simply accept the budget proposals brought by the government," says Sérgio. "They start comparing with previous years. They have the documents to do so. They have learnt. They start questioning why something else got more money than the top priority of the participatory process. Increasingly, the government has to justify itself." Being on the COP is a steep learning curve and, in order for the expertise and confidence accruing from the experience to be shared as widely as possible, seats on the COP are rotated. No one can be a COP member, or a substitute, for more that two consecutive years, though someone can stand again after two years off.

Between September and December comes a particularly intense period in the life of a COP delegate. This is when the detailed Investment Plan is drawn up, listing the works and activities chosen for that year. The municipal chamber has never rejected the COP's budget or made any damaging amendments. The Investment Plan is published annually as a vital reference document, which all regional and thematic delegates refer to as they supervise the departments carrying out the work. The government uses the Plan when it is called to account by any organ of the participatory budget.

SOMETHING MISSING

There are problems, however. Betânia Alfonsin explains that:

> The budgetary process is not enough. The COP is very powerful but it only deals with investments. You cannot plan a city just on the basis of individual investments. We have to complement it by democratizing and strengthening urban planning. If not, you can get a gulf between city planning and specific investments. An example of this lack of coordination was the expansion of

the sewerage network, which now covers more than 80
per cent of the city. This work was not accompanied by
an investment in water treatment, which has resulted in
a considerable increase of untreated sewage flowing into
the city's main water source, Lake Guaíba.

There are two related issues here. One is that planning and policy
have not caught up with the dynamic reality of the participatory
budget. The planning department was formerly the center of power
in the old administration. It was centralized finance, the city's
"works department," one super department responsible for infrastructure and planning. The PT administration broke this up in order to carry out their democratic reforms, and resentment has
lingered on. Key professional staff in the depleted planning department have been on what is essentially a long-term "go slow." The
other issue is that government departments are fragmented and un-
coordinated. There is pressure from PB plenaries in some regions
for the government to set up regular dialogue between departments.
    In Porto Alegre, improving the efficiency of government is not
the process familiar to anyone working today in local government
in the United Kingdom (the setting of tougher targets at the top
and the tightening of the control structure in the hope that those
below deliver). In the city of participatory democracy, this is turned
on its head, for it has become almost axiomatic to connect efficiency
with democracy. "We have to democratize urban planning, and we
have to do so in a comprehensive way," says Betânia. Government
leaders are aware of this problem and have encouraged the urban
planning department to embark on a major new initiative in participation. How will the new participatory structure for urban planning link to the PB? "I'm not sure. I don't think the government
know(s) either," answered Betânia. There are signs in some areas,
however, that this participatory planning is already feeding directly
into the budget process, even becoming the basis on which delegates
choose priorities.

UNDER SIEGE

The integration of urban planning and other policy areas with the PB, and the development of a stronger, participatory approach to policy issues other than new investments, have become urgent priorities. As discussed earlier in this book, the federal government has opened the national economy to the full, unrestrained impact of global deregulation, with the concomitant pressures to privatize and run down the state's social capacities. As a result, the federal government has strengthened central control over public spending and has cut the funds going back to the cities whose citizens pay the taxes. Funds going to local authorities were reduced from 17 percent of the revenue received in 1990 to 14 percent in 1999. Further cuts have happened since.

Porto Alegre cannot put up a Chinese wall, regardless of how good its policies are on job creation, health, education, infrastructure, and social security. It is under siege, part of the front line of a global economic and political war. Almost every reflex in the city's strengthened body politic has moved in the opposite direction to that of the federal government, and indeed that of most governments across the world. On the whole, governments have willingly reduced their capacity to meet the needs of their poor by, for example, cutting public spending and lowering taxes on the rich. The Popular Administration of Porto Alegre has moved against this stream, expanding its ability to fulfill its citizens' social rights by increasing its revenue through redistributive taxation, and setting up a decision-making process deliberately responsive to the needs of the poor. The power of PB has inverted the priorities of the federal government, and in the area of new investments (of which the municipality has control), it has redistributed in favor of the poor. But the PB alone cannot adequately protect against federal policies that destroy the economic ground on which its commitment to social justice stands. All it can do is engage in the wider political struggle for federal and global change—something it does with great verve and considerable human and political resources. Meanwhile, there has been not only the misery of livelihoods destroyed by political decisions taken by Fernando Henrique Cardoso in the comfort of the presidential palace in Brasília, but also the danger that the Popular Administration itself could become unintentionally complicit in imposing on local communities the burden of clearing up the unregulated market's social mess.

NOT BY INVESTMENT DECISIONS ALONE

Essentially, the logic goes like this: against the background just described, poor communities face greater and greater social problems, causing their needs to intensify. Meanwhile, the municipal council's budget to help meet these needs is cut. Its capacity for providing high-quality free services, such as childcare, health, education, and housing, is reduced. Local communities put forward projects for solving these problems themselves. The participatory budget agrees with these grassroots solutions because they fit the basic budget criteria. But what is not discussed is the quality of the service, the level of pay, how the project connects with services provided directly by the municipality, whether the need could be met in better ways, or how it will be supervised to ensure that it is providing high-quality services. Sérgio Baerlie illustrates this problem with the example of community day-care centers.

> The money that the municipal government needs to run by itself just one day-care center is enough to fund several, perhaps more than ten, day-care centers run by community associations, where labour costs are much lower. The result is that today Porto Alegre has 118 day-care centres run by community associations with funds from city hall.

Baerlie suggests there is a danger here of unintentionally accepting a neo-liberal transfer of social policy from the state to the community and in the process undermining the principle of the provision of free public services as a universal social right.

Sérgio Baerlie also has the following concerns:

> While agreements between city hall and community organizations are public and are processed on the basis of suggestions from the people, a significant number of management issues tend to be left out of public discussion. For example: how can it be guaranteed that the professionals who are hired are not relatives of the leader of the community organization? How do we approach the fact that parents often still have to pay for the service? In that case, what is a fair price? Why must some parents pay and others not, since in the few municipal day-care centers no monthly fee is charged? In other words, how can it be ensured that public money is managed in a transparent fashion and with the agreement of parents and the community?

Baerlie is stressing that it is not enough to seek to democratize the state but that social institutions outside the state must also democratize themselves. This applies to the kinds of independent projects that are funded through the PB. "No one would suggest ending agreements such as the community day-cares initiative, yet without a democratic transformation of their management, there is no challenge to the neo-liberal 'common sense,'" explains Baerlie. The other danger is that, as private corporations increasingly involve themselves, not without self-interest, in the funding of different aspects of the "social economy" from childcare to recycling, community organizations will lose autonomy, becoming less able to stand up for the rights and needs of their communities. They will become in effect minnows keeping the water clean for the big fish.

There is a growing feeling among politically minded government officials, NGO researchers, and PB delegates that policy and strategy, as distinct from simply the priorities for the investment budget, need to be both deepened and integrated. There is active support for popular processes of urban planning and economic development, as well as pressure on city hall departments to integrate their policy. Part of the answer seems to be to extend the participatory process of decision making beyond the bi-annual City Congresses, which are more consultative than decision-making and into policy development. Debates and changes are underway. Aspects of the popular administration are unusually self-reflexive for a public body, but then they are unusual public bodies. The COP, most notably, is able to learn from its failings and change. There is also an openness to criticism at the heart of the government, which is always a good sign and a contrast to the defensiveness so often found in many political authorities. For example, the mayor's office organized a seminar so that international researchers could share their criticisms.

ALL DRESSED UP AND NOWHERE TO GO: THE PARTY SEEKS A NEW DIRECTION

Traditionally the party, in this case the PT, would play the leadership role in the formation of policy and strategy for the city. It would be the party that would choose a direction, stay a step or two ahead, collectively develop a clear vision, and be, in effect, the brains behind the process. But PB has a problem, born of success: the process of participatory budgeting has proved unpredictable. In contrast to the conventional model of a party controlling, or perceiving itself to control, a state apparatus, PB has unleashed a more potent, more broadly based, means of controlling at least a central part of the state. Instead of monopolizing the role of conscious political brain, it has encouraged many political "brains" and many self-conscious agents of social change. This implicitly challenges the nature— though not the fact—of the PT's leadership, insofar as the PT acts like a conventional political party. The Brazilian Workers Party has thus moved on to ground on which few political leaders have trod.

The PT's ability to respond creatively is shaped by its history. Its containment since its inception of different ideological tendencies on the left has meant that disputes between tendencies have always played a central role in the life of the party. It has a strong belief in democracy, but this can be at the expense of a responsiveness to the new problems and policy arising out of the party's, or rather the government's and the community's, immediate experience. It is a tension between two definitions of democracy: one meaning internal norms and rules for defined ideological differences, and the other meaning an openness to and reflexivity on the innovations and problems of practice.

Participatory budgeting appears to have changed perceptions of the PT itself in Porto Alegre: its popular support has escalated. One measure of this is the continuing choice of a PT mayor in four consecutive elections, with a growing percentage of the vote. Another is the fact that, while in 1986 only 6.4 percent of the Porto Alegre population identified with the PT, research by JB-Vox Populi with significant random samples of the population in August to September 1996 shows 46 percent making this identification. The growth in PT membership in the city was also impressive: in 1990 the PT in Porto Alegre had 8,817 members; by May 2001 it had 24,033.

While the party was growing in this phenomenal way, many of the most active, experienced members were becoming part of the local government, making approximately 600 politically appointed positions in Porto Alegre's local administration (this is the normal system in local authorities in Brazil). Consequently, when the PT came to office and turned to its own supporters to join the government, about 10 percent of the local membership moved into government. This creation of a cadre of full-time policy thinkers and doers always runs the risk of creating a two-tier party. It was exacerbated by a tendency battle in which two tendencies were victorious in the competition for the mayoral team—the radical Catholics, supporting Mayor Olívio Dutra; and the Maoist-influenced tendency (now mellowed into Gramscians) supporting Deputy Mayor Tarso Genro. This left the Trotskyist-inclined tendency marginalized in government, though it is very strong in the party. This process led early in the life of the PT government to what Luciano Brunet, the experienced *petista* who worked for the CRC, described as "a rupture between party and government, which weakened the party. At times it seemed as if people in government didn't care what the party thought."

This rift is still felt. There is a growing gulf between government *petistas* and the party outside. Inside, there are intense debates but, says Luciano, "The ordinary party members can become like spectators." The weakness of the links between party and government except at election time has been emphasized, Luciano feels, by changes that make the PT like any other traditional social democratic party, with elections for delegates to conference and leading positions only once every three years. Luciano and others believe the PT should be moving in another direction, to become more pluralistic, more closely connected with the NGOs and campaigns that many *petistas* are part of anyway. "If you want to have a participatory democracy, you need a party which reflects it," concludes Luciano. In his view, if the PT is a conscious brain, it needs to adapt to the fact that in creating a source of democratic power beyond the state, it has dismantled its monopoly of radical brainpower.

THE POWER TO DELIVER

The success of PB in driving Porto Alegre's municipal administration to spend the bulk of its investment budget on making the poor neighborhoods fit to live in is clear. Most statistics indicate progress significantly ahead of other cities: 9,000 families that twelve years ago lived in shacks now have regularized brick housing; nearly the entire population (99 percent) have treated water; the sewerage system covers 86 percent of the city, compared with 46 percent in 1989; the number of students going on to university doubled between 1989 and 1995; over 50 schools have been built in the past ten years; and truancy has fallen from 9 percent to less than 1 percent. A detailed analysis of the municipal budget after 1989 shows that the lower the average income of the PB region, the higher the volume of public investment per head. The report concludes that the participatory budget has functioned as "a powerful instrument of the redistribution of wealth."

There are also examples of the participatory budget strengthening the hand of the municipality to gain social benefits for the city from private investors. A good example of how PB was used as a launching pad to bargain for social improvements is the agreement with one of the largest European supermarket chains. In the early 1990s, the French company Carrefour wanted to build one of its supermarkets in the north-central region of Porto Alegre. This region has many small businesses, especially shops, and these small entrepreneurs were extremely angry. With the example of PB on their doorstep, they reacted by organizing a lively public meeting and decided to take their concerns to the thematic PB plenary of the budget on economic policy. "We wanted to set up a committee to negotiate for compensation for the small businesses in the area, as a condition of the new supermarket," said one of the activists. "The participatory budget was the obvious channel for this proposal."

The outcome was unprecedented. Carrefour had never before had to make real concessions to gain entry into a new marketplace. While normally its supermarkets let spaces inside for around twenty local shops, the Porto Alegre committee won an agreement for forty. The company also agreed to employ young people, since they are the ones suffering most from high unemployment, and to help fund training schemes. In the past, the government had successfully bargained for infrastructural improvements from transnationals, such as McDonalds, but it had never before obtained social improvements. It seems likely that the small entrepreneurs gained confidence, moral clout, and political backing through discussing their demands and winning the support of the participatory budget.

CONCLUSIONS: A NEW BACKBONE
FOR DEMOCRACY

In one sense, the civic power that has emerged around the participatory budget depends on the state being willing to share power.
There would not be the sustained levels of participation, the popular
basis for this civic power, if there were not significant public resources at stake. However, the new source of power that develops
once this condition is in place has a life and dynamic of its own,
which Porto Alegre's local state respects and supports. The rules and
meetings of the participatory budget institutionalize its independence and protect it against unilateral action by the state.

The transparency and publicly negotiated character of the rules
for PB ensure that it is widely respected and supported. It is perceived to have a legitimacy distinct from the electoral institutions of
the mayor and the municipal assembly. The government cannot
change PB rules by its own authority. Instead everything must be
negotiated in a process that, until the last legal moment of agreeing
the budget, is heavily weighted toward the popular participants.
Now, after twelve years of PB, to close the process down would
provoke an eruption. And not just in the poor parts of town. PB is
an extension of democracy, not a competing structure. It effectively
makes the mayor's electoral mandate a daily living pressure on the
state apparatus.

Conventionally, elected representatives delegate detailed investment decisions to unelected administrators. In this respect, PB is
morally more legitimate than representative structures. Added to this
moral power is detailed knowledge, so that municipal councillors and
the mayor are no longer dependent only on technical staff but have
democratic allies with inside local knowledge who can challenge the
administration if it is inefficient or corrupt. This combination of democratic legitimacy and practical knowledge is proving desirable in
other areas of the administration as well. Participatory decision making has turned out to be a more socially efficient way of running
things, delivering a better city to live in.

The democratic legitimacy and valuing of practical knowledge inherent in participatory processes also has the power to strengthen civic power in relation to the private sector. In cases like Carrefour, the participatory process was able to call capitalism's bluff precisely because the legitimacy and longevity of liberal capitalism is rooted in a proclaimed respect for democracy. Big companies rarely claim overtly that, because they have got the money, they can do what they like. The problem is that democracy rarely puts capitalism to the test. Democracy is more often than not on its knees. In a relatively thriving commercial city like Porto Alegre, it need not be. As a desirable location for investment, it has considerable bargaining power.

It is not an easy or quick process to construct the kind of participatory democracy practiced in Porto Alegre. In 1998, the PT won the elections for the government of Rio Grande do Sul, the state that has Porto Alegre as its capital. The new government began to extend PB across the state but faced resistance in many rural areas still dominated by reactionary landowners. It was unable to get the system running as effectively as it had hoped. As a result of this and other factors (including bickering between different *petista* factions), the PT lost the state government elections in Rio Grande do Sul in October 2002, as mentioned earlier. It was a bitter disappointment for the local *petistas*, tempering their delight at Lula's triumph.

GLOSSARY

Aliança de Libertação Nacional (ALN) National Liberation Alliance

Central Única dos Trabalhadores (CUT) Workers Unified Confederation

Comissão Pastoral da Terra (CPT) Pastoral Land Commission

Comunidade Eclesial de Base (CEB) Catholic Grassroots Community

Movimento Democrático Brasilero (MDB) Brazilian Democratic Movement

Movimento dos Trabalhadores Rurais Sem Terra (MST) Landless Rural Workers Movement

Partido Comunista Brasileiro (PCB) Brazilian Communist Party

Partido Comunista Brasileiro Revolucionário (PCBR) Revolutionary Brazilian Communist Party

Partido Comunista do Brasil (PCdoB) Communist Party of Brazil

Partido do Movimento Democrático Brasileiro (PMDB) Brazilian Democratic Movement Party

Partido dos Trabalhadores (PT) Workers Party

Partido Socialista Brasileiro (PSB) Brazilian Socialist Party

Partido Socialista dos Trabalhadores Unificado (PSTU) Unified Workers Socialist Party

NOTES

CHAPTER 1

1. This chapter incorporates firsthand description of election night by Jan Rocha. See NACLA (North American Congress on Latin America) on www.nacla.org.
2. Interview done by the PT and published on its website, *Lula Presidente*.
3. In an interview with the Argentine newspaper, *Clarin*, 29 September 2002.
4. *Folha de S. Paulo*, 13 November 2002.

CHAPTER 2

1. Margaret E. Keck, *The Workers Party and Democratization in Brazil* (New Haven, CT: Yale University Press, 1991).
2. The main groups that joined the PT were Socialist Democracy (Democracia Socialista), a Trotskyist group, affiliated to the Fourth International, which wanted to transform the PT into a revolutionary Marxist party; Socialist Convergence (Convergência Socialista), also Trotskyist, which aimed to transform the PT into a mass Marxist party; the small group, Movement for the Emancipation of the Proletariat (Movimento de Emancipação do Proletariado, or MEP); the PCBR (split from the PCdoB) and the APML, both of which saw the PT as a transitional party and a recruiting ground; Libelu, a faction of the

Fourth International, which aimed to take control of the new party.

3. Partido dos Trabalhadores, *Resoluções de Encontros e Congressos (Conference and Congress Resolutions)* (editora Fundação Perseu Abramo), São Paulo, 1998.

4. Emir Sader, *Quando novos personagens entram em cena* (São Paulo: Paz e Terra, 1988).

5. Including Frei Betto, Plínio de Arruda Sampaio, and Irma Passoni.

6. Pelego is the cowhide that horsemen put underneath the saddle to absorb the impact caused when horse and rider are in motion or, as it is used here, to stop it rubbing a sore patch on the horse's skin.

7. ABC is the name given to the industrial belt outside São Paulo, made up of the municipal districts of Santo André, São Bernardo, and São Caetano.

8. Known as the Thesis of Lins. For this and other documents about the history of the PT, see The Workers Party, *Resoluções de Encontros e Congressos*.

9. Among the founders and first leaders of the party were Apolônio de Carvalho, Mario Pedrosa, Manoel da Conceição, Sérgio Buarque de Holanda, Moacyr Gadotti, Antônio Cândido, Florestan Fernandes, Paul Singer, Francisco Weffort, José Ibrahim, Helena Greco, and Paulo Freire.

10. Partido dos Trabalhadores, *Resoluções de Encontros e Congressos*.

11. Ibid.; PT Political Action and Organisational Plan 1986–1988 (Plano de Ação Política e Organizativa do PT para o Período 1986–1988), São Paulo: Editora Fundação Perseu Abramo, 1998.

12. Convergencia Socialista formed its own party, the Unified Socialist Workers Party (Partido Socialista dos Trabalhadores Unificado, or PSTU), which supported Lula in the 1994 campaign.

13. The main tendencies on the eve of the 1994 campaign were Left Choice (Opção à esquerda) (33 percent), formed by Democracia Socialista and members of the ALN such as Ruy Falcão; Unity in Struggle (Unidade na Luta) (31 percent), formed by trade

union leaders such as Lula and Olívio Dutra; In the Struggle (Na Luta) (20 percent), orthodox Marxist tendency formed by Sokol and Greenhalgh; Democracia Radical (11 percent), parliamentary social democrats, formed by Eduardo Jorge and José Genoíno; and independents, such as Francisco Weffort and other intellectuals.

14. Articulação elected 33 percent of delegates. The PT in Struggle (Na Luta PT) group, formed by the Trotskyist group Labour (O Trabalho) and deputy Luis Eduardo Greenhalgh, elected 20 percent of delegates. The party began to be run jointly by these tendencies. To the right, the Radical Democracy (Democracia Radical), formed mainly by members of Congress, elected only 11 percent of delegates; other tendencies and independents elected the remaining delegates.

15. The main ones were Democracia Socialista, affiliated to Mandel's Fourth International; Redoing (Refazendo), led by the Rio de Janeiro federal deputy, Milton Temer; and Network (Rede), led by the ex-mayor of Porto Alegre, Tarso Genro, who was considered a possible PT presidential candidate. Other groups, such as O Trabalho, continued to exist.

16. A resolution at the party's First Congress spoke of the "need to build a broad network of social and popular movements; to permit the combination of the most varied forms of struggle and links between urban and rural areas; and the construction of a political and social bloc and the dispute of hegemony." Partido dos Trabalhadores, *Resoluções de Encontros e Congressos*, pp. 479 ff.

17. All routine political decisions are voted on by the twenty-one members of the National Executive Commission, which meets regularly. More important decisions go to meetings of the eighty-six-member National Directorate. Strategic or ideological issues are discussed in Conferences, held every two years, or at Congress, held every five years. Congress has the same rigorous format as the major socialist parties had at the beginning of the twentieth century.

18. Partido dos Trabalhadores, *Resoluções de Encontros e Congressos*, pp. 479 ff.
19. Ibid.

CHAPTER 3

1. Quoted in Sue Branford and Bernardo Kucinski, *Carnival of the Oppressed — Lula and the Brazilian Workers Party* (London: Latin America Bureau, 1995), p. 34.

CHAPTER 4

1. See Fernando Henrique Cardoso, *Mudanças Sociais na América Latina* (São Paulo: Difusão Européia do Livro, 1969); and F. H. Cardoso and Enzo Faletto, *Dependency and Development in Latin America* (Berkeley, 1979).
2. Geisa Maria Rocha, "Neo-Dependency in Brazil," *New Left Review* 16 (July–August 2002): 32.
3. Luiz Carlos Bresser-Pereira, "Financiamento para o Subdesenvolvimento: o Brasil e o Segundo Consenso de Washington," paper presented during the conference commemorating the fiftieth anniversary of the creation of the Banco Nacional de Desenvolvimento Econômico e Social (BNDES), 14 October 2002, p. 15.
4. Rocha, "Neo-Dependency in Brazil," 7.
5. Quoted in ibid., 8.
6. Ibid.
7. Harry Shutt, *The Trouble with Capitalism: An Enquiry into the Causes of Global Economic Failure* (London and New York: Zed Books, 1998), p. 82.
8. Rocha, "Neo-Dependency in Brazil," 9.
9. UNCTAD, *World Investment Report 2001*, Country Fact Sheet (Brazil, Geneva: UNCTAD).

10. Bresser-Pereira, *Financiamento para o Subdesenvolvimento*, 24.
11. Ibid., 19.
12. Rocha, "Neo-Dependency in Brazil," 9.
13. This did not happen when Argentina defaulted in December 2001, as the U.S. government wanted to show it could be tough with "irresponsible debtors" and so did not support a further bail-out; but even then the foreign banks did not bear heavy losses, as the Argentine collapse was so widely predicted that foreign banks had already taken out most of their money by the time it actually happened.
14. Figures from IPEA (Instituto de Pesquisa Econômica Aplicada).
15. This program was implemented by the then Health Minister, José Serra, later to run as the ruling party's presidential candidate in the 2002 election. Serra's tough stance on Brazil's right to produce its own generic drugs greatly angered the powerful US pharmaceutical multinationals. In 2002 several US newspapers reported that the US administration was more hostile to Serra than to Lula, who had earned grudging respect within the US tradition of self-made men.
16. See chapter 9 in Sue Branford and Jan Rocha, *Cutting the Wire: the Story of the Landless Movement in Brazil* (London: Latin America Bureau, 2002).
17. Figures from Instituto Brasileiro de Geografia e Estadística (IBGE).
18. Quoted in Altamiro Borges, "A Regressão do Trabalho na 'Era FHC,'" *Revista Mensal* 2 (16 September 2002).
19. Ibid.
20. Ibid.
21. Ibid.
22. *Folha de S. Paulo*, 13 May 2001.
23. ECLAC, *Social Panorama*, Table 11.2, ECLAC, pp. 70–1.
24. See chapter 12 in Branford and Rocha, *Cutting the Wire*.
25. *Financial Times*, 15 October 2002.

26. *Financial Times*, 10 November 2002.
27. Shutt, *The Trouble with Capitalism*, 82.
28. Harry Shutt, *A New Democracy: Alternatives to a Bankrupt World Order*, (London and New York: Global Issues Series, Zed Books, 2001).
29. *Folha de S. Paulo*, 1 November 2002.
30. Roger Burbach, *Brazil's Lula: Confounding Friends and Foes*, paper circulated on the Internet, June 2003.
31. Interview with João Pedro Stédile, in *Revista PUC-VIVA* 19 (São Paulo: Feb-April 2003).

CHAPTER 5

1. This is an edited and shortened version of a chapter of *Reclaim the State: Experiments in People's Democracy*, by Hilary Wainwright (London and New York: Verso, 2003).
2. Since my visit, this cycle has been modified so that there is now just one round of public assemblies where the regional delegates and budget councillors are elected and the thematic priorities are chosen. The "single round," as it is now called, is preceded by many meetings where the municipal government is called to account for the past year and people begin the debates about priorities and criteria for the election of delegates for the regional fora and the budget council.

BIBLIOGRAPHY

Branford, Sue, and Bernardo Kucinski. *Carnival of the Oppressed: Lula and the Brazilian Workers Party*. London: Latin America Bureau, 1995.

Branford, Sue, and Jan Rocha. *Cutting the Wire: The Story of the Landless Movement in Brazil*. London: Latin America Bureau, 2002.

Harnecker, Marta. *O Sonho era Possível*. São Paulo: MEPLA, Casa América Livre, 1994.

Keck, Margaret. *The Workers Party and Democratization in Brazil*. New Haven: Yale University Press, 1992.

Resoluções de Encontros e Congressos (Conference and Congress Resolutions). *Partido dos Trabalhadores*. São Paulo: Editora Fundação Perseu Abramo, 1998.

Sader, Emir. *Quando Novos Personagens Entram em Cena*. São Paulo: Paz e terra, 1988.

Sader, Emir, and Ken Silverstein. *Without Fear of Being Happy: Lula, the Workers Party and Brazil*. London and New York: Verso, 1991.

Shutt, Harry. *The Trouble with Capitalism: An Enquiry into the Causes of Global Economic Failure*. London and New York: Zed Books, 1998.

Shutt, Harry. *A New Democracy: Alternatives to a Bankrupt World Order*. London and New York: Global Issues Series, Zed Books, 2001.

Souza Martins, José de. *O Poder do Atraso: Ensaios de Sociologia da História Lenta*. São Paulo: Editora Hucitec, 1999.

Wainwright, Hilary. *Reclaim the State, Adventures in Popular Democracy*. London and New York: Verso, 2003.

About the Authors

Sue Branford spent ten years in Brazil where she reported for the *Financial Times*, *The Economist*, and the *Observer*. After returning to London she worked for the BBC. She has written books on Brazil and Latin America. Her latest book, which she co-authored with Jan Rocha, is *Cutting the Wire: The Story of the Landless Movement in Brazil*.

Bernardo Kucinski is currently an advisor in President Lula's Social Communications Department in Brasília. He lectures in journalism at the School of Communications and Arts at the University of São Paulo. He previously worked as a journalist for *Veja*, the BBC, *Gazeta Mercantil*, *Exame*, and most of the alternative newspapers of the 1970s (some of which he helped to found), and was the *Guardian* correspondent in Brazil for many years. He is the author of several books, including *Brazil: Carnival of the Oppressed* (with Sue Branford).

Hilary Wainwright is the editor of the green left monthly magazine, *Red Pepper*, and writes regularly for the *Guardian*. She is a research fellow at the International Labour Studies Centre, Manchester, UK, and Fellow of the Transnational Institute, Amsterdam. Her books include *Arguments for a New Left: Answering the Free Market Right*, and several books on radical trade unionism and economic democracy. Her latest book is *Reclaim the State: Experiments in People's Democracy*.